DEATH
of a
NIGHTINGALE

2022

ALAN SHARE

Copyright © 2023 Alan Share with *i*spy from a Blog edited by Jan Woolf.

All rights reserved. No part of this book may be reproduced in any form or by any electronic or mechanical means, including information storage and retrieval systems, without permission in writing from the author and publisher, except by reviewers, who may quote brief passages in a review.

ISBN: 978-1-961096-05-9 (Paperback Edition)
ISBN: 978-1-961096-06-6 (Hardcover Edition)
ISBN: 978-1-961096-04-2 (E-book Edition)

Book Ordering Information

The Regency Publishers, International
7 Bell Yard London WO2A2JR

info@theregencypublishers.com
www.theregencypublishers.international
+44 20 8133 0466

Printed in the United States of America

In Memory of my mother, Esther

When you meet your friend on the roadside or in the market place, let your spirit in you move your lips and direct your tongue.
Let the voice within your voice speak to the ear of his ear.
For his soul will keep the truth of your heart as the taste of the wine is remembered
When the colour is forgotten and the vessel is no more.

The Prophet - Kahlil Gibran

Contents

2022 vii
Preface xiii
Prologue xvii

Death of a Nightingale 1
   Programme Note 1
   Cast & crew 4
   Act One 12
   Act two 38

The Mad Hatter's Committee Meeting 56

*i*spy – Extracts from a Blog, edited by Jan Woolf 61
Notes & Quotes 118
   1 An OFSTED Report on a Special School 2010 118
   2 An Exposé - the origins of Inclusion in the UK 119
   3 The Case for Inclusion - The Salamanca Statement 123
   4 Defective Academic Research 124
   5 The dream turns sour! 126
   6 Alarm bells ring 128
   7 A change of policy 132
   8 Rights 134
   9 Pupil perceptions 134
   10 The System 135
   11 God - A Universal Creator 136
   12 Music and the Mind 142
   13 Equality 143
   14 Pills 143
   15 The Dome 145

16 School Organisation Committees 145
17 The Luddites 145
18 Helen Keller 146

Questions for Quiet Contemplation 148
The clash of human rights and "Unequal Opportunity" 150
Freedom of Expression in the UK Today? 162
Bibliography 171
A Testimonial of Substance 174
Alan Share 176

2022

I published Death of a Nightingale in 2011. It was my protest. I had witnessed the unsuccessful attempt of a local authority to close a special school for children with a physical disability and a learning difficulty against the wishes of the parents, teachers, carers, its pupils and the doctors who cared for them. The lengths they were prepared to go to, the closure of over 100 special schools in the UK was the provocation.

Today, I have to record that the school is still there, but it now caters for students aged 11-19 years with an Autistic Spectrum Disorder or complex learning difficulties. Its hydrotherapy pool is no longer required.

The rights of parents of children similar to the ones that I knew no longer exist. Their children are in mainstream schools, probably bullied, with well-meaning support, but from NTAs not from nurses and physios with hydrotherapy and from teachers with the time that they need.

Today, I see that this story is part of a larger story.

First, what should happen when human rights clash? Here Parliament had provided the right of children to mainstream education. It had also provided the right to parents of children with special needs to the school of their choice. Here every single one of them wanted a special school.

The word Equality doesn't help here. It makes mischief! Only fair play works. Sadly, I witnessed its total absence.

I studied Jurisprudence at Oxford. I still recall the lectures on human rights given by the eminent, widely respected Professor Herbert Hart. He cautioned the way you should use the word "right", sometimes legally right, sometimes morally right but not a legal entitlement, sometimes simply "wouldn't it be nice if". I do not recall him asking the question as to what should happen when human rights clash as here.

In my own life I have witnessed it on several occasions. One person's right to strike and another person's right to work. One person's right to protest and another person's right to use the public highway. My right to free expression and a lawyer's right to protect his reputation compromised by it truthfully and fairly.

The word equality is no help here. Rights are not equal and absolute. They are relative and different.

I suggest that when human rights conflict, fair play, is the only solvent.

In the Clash of Human Rights and "Unequal Opportunity" I show you what happens when brute political power fortified by dogma and soundbite is the arbiter, and the media don't interfere.

Also, in the last ten years I have realised that what I write about in relation to children with special educational needs applies equally to many other children as well, half a primary school cohort that for one reason or another does not go to university. Success and fulfilment in life does not need a degree nor does a degree guarantee it.

To be the best you can be in a fast-changing world as Michelle Obama urged pupils on a visit to England, needs an education that facilitates that. A curriculum designed to provide an opportunity to go to Uni, is not that.

I have listened to Sir Ken Robinson on YouTube. Sadly, he died a year ago and I write this in his memory. I write this up in my new book MY ENGLAND. Currently the law of copyright prevents its publication.

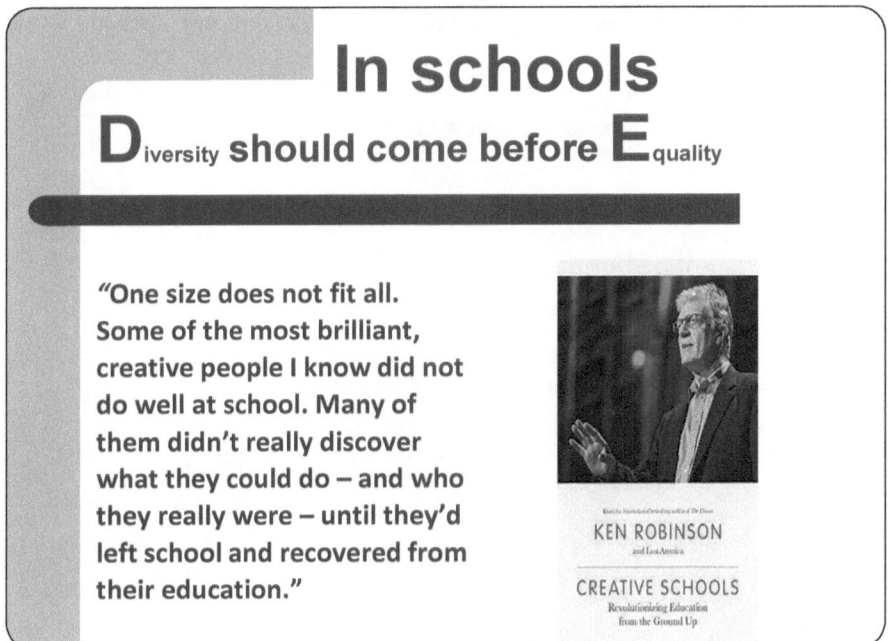

So, I pose here two questions.

Are some people so eager to give children an equal opportunity to go to university that they largely ignore the needs of all those who cannot or do not want to go there? They can have successful and fulfilling lives without it, with no student debt to carry for their working lives. Shouldn't they have a curriculum suited to their needs in a fast-changing challenging world, and exams they can pass with flying colours?

And are they so fixated on equality and the mantra words "inclusion" and "parity of esteem" for some, that they ignore self-esteem that teachers should try to nurture in all their pupils? No wonder there are skill shortages.

Diversity should always come before Equality in education and the pursuit of excellence should apply to everyone.

I have just seen on my TV an advert promoting mental health: *"Almost half of the young struggle with anxiety."* And in Michelle Obama's latest book *The Light We Carry* I read *"Real growth begins with how gladly you're able to see yourself."* Teachers, please bin the words "Parity of Esteem". Your job is to nurture "Self-esteem" and a sense of achievement. And the world will look after itself.

Thinking time, as you read this book.

Death of a Nightingale

with *i spy – Extracts from a Blog, edited by Jan Woolf*
and *Alice in Blunderland – The Mad Hatters' Committee meeting*

Alan Share

Adapted for a stage performance at the New End Theatre, New End, Hampstead, London
9 March – 3 April 2011

Directed by Thomas Scott

Preface

Back in 1988 I was a local business man, and a member of my local Rotary Club. I was persuaded, as an act of Rotary service, to become a Governor of a Special School for physically disabled children with an associated learning difficulty. A year later I became its Chair of Governors, a position I held until 2002.

This was to change my life and apart from anything else, help to turn me into something of a writer - a very great surprise that I did not expect.

At Merton College, Oxford, I had planned to become a barrister, and to the extent that once a barrister always a barrister, I still am. My career at the Bar in Manchester was to last for only three years. Manchester came and went.

I was won over by Jo Grimond's inspirational leadership of the Liberal Party, and I moved from the Bar to the Head Office of the Party in Victoria Street, London, as Executive Assistant to its Secretary. In those days the Government, as Jo Grimond once chided it, "couldn't run a sweetie shop in the Lothian Road". Would they manage it any better today? Some things have not changed very much over the years. Therein lies a part of the problem. Anyway, I worked there for three years before joining a family furniture company. I had tried to avoid that but, as it turned out, I was to enjoy the ride, and stay with it until I retired. So far as the Liberal Party was concerned, I had walked with Jo Grimond "towards the sound of gunfire", but I never quite got there - nor, I fear, did he.

It is amazing how you can misread things when you are young.

I don't, however, begrudge either of my early short lived work experiences. Both of them were learning experiences. Building bricks, I call them.

On the Northern Circuit I was privileged to have as Head of Chambers, and as my pupil master, the late C.N.Glidewell, CNG to everyone who knew him. He was a man with old fashioned integrity. He was also a master of advocacy - particularly good when he showed up the ineptitude of local planners. He also had style. All of this was somehow encapsulated in his choice of car - a *Bristol* - a prestigious saloon engineered with traditional British quality in its design. In all ways CNG was a cut above the ordinary.

The Law taught me the importance of two things. Firstly keep everything in writing. I have paid a heavy price for that. And secondly keep as far away from lawyers as possible. I have not always been successful in this, and sadly have found that a few can best be described as little more than gas meters constantly demanding to be fed. Not all merit that description, and I do exempt my own solicitor here.

My experience of politics encouraged me to keep as far away as possible from that too. But this has never been an easy thing for me to do.

Becoming a Governor was the start of my serious writing - a diary to keep a written record of everything. Letters, memoranda, and emails, you name it, I wrote them, and copied them into my diary. This is now ancient history.

I must record one other youthful mistake. I used to imagine that the world was a rational place. My wife, who had studied psychology at Newcastle University, put me right. I suddenly realised that reasoning usually starts in the gut, not in the brain. At Oxford, Roman law, not psychology, had been an important part of my course in Jurisprudence. A pity since this revelation has changed my way of thinking - and of writing ever since.

It has influenced the way that I have processed many words in the last twenty years.

Allow me to explain. Over a hundred special schools have been closed in recent years as successive governments moved more and more children with special needs into mainstream schools. The buzz word here was 'Inclusion'. The future of the school I was associated with was uncertain for many years. Parents who fought to keep it open were swimming against a strongly running tide that constantly threatened to engulf it.

It would have been a great shame to close it because it was a very good school, and it certainly wasn't cut off from the outside world. This was not just my view of it - OFSTED was of the same opinion. I have now seen a very similar report for Oak Lodge School in East Finchley that provided actors for my play.[1]

I still have snapshots of the school in my mind from the time I joined it as Governor in 1988. A head teacher with a vision and a mission statement shared with his deputy "*Whole School - Whole Child*", warm, dedicated and committed staff, and above all bright eyed, happy purposeful children, enjoying their school days and helping each other along the way. A win, win situation for everyone included in it - parents, teachers, carers and most of all its pupils. Presentation Evenings captured it all. That is where they all came together in one joyous, celebratory event. They all had the pride of achievement - without being proud.

The parents were successful in their campaign to keep the school open and it is still in existence today.

I couldn't have written Death of a Nightingale without that in the background, but it is not that story. I must stress that it is a piece of fiction. I dedicate it to all those people working with special needs, to children with special needs and to their parents. I came to have a huge respect for all of them. In their interests I would like to combat the stigma that moves towards Inclusion have, at times, wrongly attached to special schools. This is important since the tide towards a policy that was based upon the dogma of Inclusion and not upon its practicability and its suitability, is now on the turn.

There is a growing awareness that inclusive education is not appropriate for all children with special education needs. The Coalition Government issued a Green Paper in March 2001 stating that the bias towards mainstream schools should be ended.

The book as I published it in 2008 is now out of date. The play I wrote "to be read" has now been performed at the New End Theatre in Hampstead earlier in the year. It is shorter, better and different. I hope you will watch edited versions of it on my website. The Prologue in the book remains unaltered.

Prologue

We shall not cease from exploration
And the end of all our exploring
Will be to arrive where we started
And know the place for the first time.

TS Eliot, Four Quartets, Little Gidding 1942

I believe in a Creator, though many do not. But I cannot see some great figure sitting astride the Universe with all its galaxies determining everything, and I cannot see someone that I can personally talk to. So I can live with ritual; but prayer is more difficult. I am envious of Emma Kirk, the music teacher in the play, who has that facility. When she finally meets her Maker, she will do so with equanimity. I hope you will warm to her as I do.

My route to my Creator is through my relationship with man, and with an awesome awareness of the incredible wonders of the Universe, of which man is but a tiny part. For me God does not replicate the attributes of man. That would deny us our freewill. And we would all be puppets on his string. Whether we are believers or non-believers we must surely not be puppets.

There is a price to be paid for that. For good or for ill, we have a choice. We can be saints or sinners, and there has never been a shortage of either. Starting way back in the Garden of Eden - or just in the distant past - we were given personal choice in our lives as our birthright. This is one of the things this book is about. How we exercise it, and how much of it we are actually allowed to exercise in the 21st Century. If you see personal choice as a bourgeois fad, you cancel out personal responsibility too, and herald authoritarianism. Is that what you want?

Fate steps in

Despite all that I think that some things have to happen. Providence takes a hand. This Prologue was the result.

Consider the following coincidence and its consequences. I am in Manhattan for a number of reasons. One is to see old friends, not least to see a beautiful lady, now in her nineties. I met her almost fifty years ago when she welcomed me to her home as a guest of her somewhat eccentric son. He must have been more than a bit eccentric. He wrote from New York offering his services to the British Liberal Party. I was also a bit eccentric at the time. I was working in Victoria Street, and I replied to his letter, asking him to call in. This was the start of many treasured trans-Atlantic friendships that I have come to enjoy.

The other reason I am in New York is to look at works of art. I have seized a rare opportunity to look in wonder at Gustav Klimt's *Adele Block-Bauer I* at the Neu Galerie, and I am in a café enjoying a cup of coffee. I notice at the next table a short, stocky, bespectacled, well dressed but somewhat crumpled very senior citizen. What took my eye was that he was tucking in to a large piece of chocolate cake, a huge mound of cream, and an ice cream sundae. He was also sporting four colourful badges on his dark professional suit as well as a very lively tie and something else, which I cannot make out, dangling round his neck. This was not an everyday occurrence, even in New York.

We got into conversation and I discovered he was a retired doctor and a wise, interesting and probably lonely old bird. He had a very dry sense of humour that I warmed to. As he drew upon his reservoir of quip and anecdote, his serious face melted into a smile that was both benign and mischievous, a true raconteur. He was also a flirt with the ladies. We invited him to join us that evening for a meal, and to our great pleasure he did. I thought it would be lovely to introduce this great character to my American hostess of yesteryear. It was an idea that appeared to die a death.

Quite a few days later I was walking through Central Park on my way to see my ninety year old lady friend. As I walked down Park Avenue, who should I see but the same crumpled up character clutching a paper parcel in one hand and a broken down walking stick in the other emerging from an apartment. A moment earlier, a moment later, I would have missed him. I invited him to come with me. And so we walked at something less than a snail's pace to our destination, stopping only to enable him to talk to every doorman en route, reminding them of his former patients in that particular apartment block, and to catch his breath.

As we walked we discussed many things. His father had been one of the founders of the American Liberal Party. I didn't know that one existed. I shared with him my view as to the Achilles heel of the Liberal - naiveté. An endearing quality if you recognise it, a very dangerous one if you don't. "Insanity," he said. He reminded me of King Lear. We were on the same wavelength.

When we reached my friend's apartment, we discussed the play and the background to it, and I read out a few extracts. She had already read most of it. She said that she liked it, but that from time to time it had lost its way. At this point my newly found friend and admirer urged me to consider the methodology of George Bernard Shaw, write a Prologue and put into it the generalities of the thoughts provoked in me by my writing. I could then leave them out of the play almost altogether. This actually tied in with some other helpful advice from another quarter. This friend had identified parts of my writing as "rant". She had liked the rest.

"Rant", of course, is a word some people use to dismiss thoughts and ideas that they cannot go along with. But she was right. I needed another seedbed for them. A Prologue suddenly made sense to help my readers on their way.

If you want to understand the writing, you need to have some understanding of the writer, and where the writing comes from. I am interested in the microcosm, and I am interested in the whole of which the microcosm reflects.

So here are the thoughts behind the play. The bee - or bees - in my bonnet that refuse to fly away. The assumptions, I suggest, that shouldn't always be assumed, that I invite you to question. A play focussing on a school for children with Special Educational Needs provides me with a vehicle in which to travel the world. Come and join me on my journey.

The play is set in a special school. So, firstly, here are my thoughts about Special Educational Needs, about the policy of Inclusion in Education and about the right to it. Just why, despite all the paper plans, despite all the talk of human rights, why do they continue to get it wrong? Why do they fail to give so many children the one chance they have?

Inclusion or disillusion?

Rights! My mind goes back to a lecture by Herbert Hart, the eminent Professor of Jurisprudence at Oxford. He explained that there was not one single meaning for the word "right". There could be five or more different meanings depending on how it was used. In addition "rights" are not always complementary to each other and they are rarely, if ever, absolute.

Sometimes one person's "right" - say a UK citizen's right to live in safety and not to be blown up by a propane gas bomb loaded with nails - or to have a fear of this - may conflict with the rights of migrants seeking to enter this country. You have to be very careful how you use the word "right". You need fine judgment and, as Professor Hart argued, a sense of fair play in deciding when and how to assert it. It is just as well to remember that while human rights may enable lawyers pronouncing on them to enjoy the fruits of Utopia; they allow the rest of us only a partial glimpse of it. In Professor Hart's own words human rights are "the prime philosophical inspiration of political and social reform"[8]. Often they are no more than that.

So, when you talk about the "right" to Inclusive Education you should recognise that some will want to assert it and may succeed and thrive. Some may assert it but be disappointed and wish they hadn't. Some may want to assert it but be denied it. Finally, some may not want to assert it at all but be forced to accept it with no other realistic choice available, and some may want to assert a different right altogether - the right to go to a special school. Remember that children without special needs have their rights too. This actually summarises how things are.

Social reformers have not always grasped this. I suspect that many have looked at this simplistically, seeing it as essentially society's difficulty not an individual's, and projecting what they *felt in their gut* they would want for *themselves* for everyone else, a weakness that is not always wise. Even disability organisations that have done so much to help the disabled may have fallen into the same trap. That is why they may not always have seen the quite different and varying needs that some children and their parents actually have, and a not always pleasant reality they have to deal with every single day. Very simply, some do not want an open door. What they want is a helping hand and the comfort zone of their own company. For them change is a worry and a threat.

Inclusion is a concept that is absolutely wonderful in the libraries of the mind. It is not always quite so wonderful in the classrooms of the real world, especially if vulnerable children are excluded when they are supposed to be included, made to feel unwanted and, at its worst, shoehorned into a hostile environment.[5]

Today classrooms are populated by far too many bully boys and girls. Teachers may have too little time and sometimes too little training as well. Supply teachers are here today and gone tomorrow. Teaching assistants don't always know how to stretch children in the way that trained teachers do and, in many cases, do not improve attainment. Ironically they can create a sense of exclusion in an inclusive environment, stigmatising pupils in the process. Teachers are not always trained to relate to them. Thousands more teaching assistants have come on stream since 1997, quite a number of them supporting children with special needs. Did anyone anticipate this - and calculate the cost? In addition, there are too few therapists and money is still short. But then the policy of Inclusion was never properly costed by anyone in the first place. Thus, cost benefit analysis is a totally alien concept.

It is far too simplistic and naïve, to say that the failure of the plans can be attributed to the shortage of money. If that is the case, then in the nature of things they will be destined always to fail. Fortunately there is more hope than that if people realise it. This is not just about money. It is about *the way* that money is spent, *who* spends it, and *where* it is spent. You don't solve problems simply by throwing money at them. The very first thing you have to do is to try to understand the problems.

What I sense children with special needs and their parents want is not sympathy but understanding and compassion. You express sympathy, but you feel compassion, a very important distinction.

This is another reason why well-intentioned plans have failed. Compassion can never be part of the job description of civil servants. Even empathy may be too much to ask. Central government is too remote, and local government is too notoriously parsimonious. Neither is best structured to deal with something that would better be handled by authorities that are regional and accountable. Airports are managed this way.

Just how sensitive is the system today to individual needs that are far more numerous and varied than most people realise? Does it even begin to think in terms of a holistic approach to learning difficulties? I pose these questions.

Education should be about preparing children to be included in society as adults. One form of education does not fit all children, and it is very unwise to believe that it does.

Therefore I present *Death of a Nightingale*. In the pursuit of inclusion, your social engineer has all too often put square pegs into round holes ... with Araldite. He does so whenever he goes against the grain of man's natural instincts, and because his focus is on outcomes, and not on meeting individual needs. He does not know what those needs are, nor does he feel any need to know. He combines myopia with tunnel vision. Society then has to cope with the consequences. This, however, is just square one.

Where does control stop and participation begin?

Many teachers are highly committed to their job, but they have too many things asked of them that get in the way, and not enough time and energy to do it all. Then there are all those working in the public service who feel obliged to do some things they know they shouldn't be doing, or not do things that they should. There are school governors, and people like them, who are doing valuable voluntary work within the community, but who are deliberately denied the tools to do it properly by those who prefer to do it themselves, but want to make it look otherwise.

It is the System that needs looking at, the con in consultation, the charade of partnership, the make-believe, and as a result, the mess of much of it.[10]

I am only saying here what more and more people are saying. Lying has become endemic from the top downwards. But when proven lying is a heinous crime in our society. the denial and the cover-up necessarily follow, and compound the initial problem. The checks and balances that I always thought were an integral part of a democratic society have been disabled. If there is a cock-up, heads should just occasionally roll. They do in the private sector.

In 2006 The Institute for Public Policy Research issued a publication entitled *Whitehall's Black Box: Accountability and Performance in the Senior Civil Service*. Here is one quotation from it. "*What, then, is precisely wrong with the way Whitehall is governed? This is best put by saying that lines of accountability are weak and confused. There is a 'governance vacuum' at the heart of Whitehall.*"

I pose the question in the context of education for special needs. Is the System of government providing an education that enables children to rise to the challenges of the 21st Century? It needs to look at itself in the mirror. Read Rudi Giuliani's book entitled *Leadership*. This is what he says about education in New York City: *"What the system should have been about was educating its million children as well as possible. Instead it existed to provide jobs for the people who worked in it, and to preserve those Jobs regardless of performance."* Could the criticism apply to this country as well?

The recent *Power Report* pointed to *"the weakening of effective dialogue between governed and governors"* and *"the rise of quiet authoritarianism within government."* If I can remove the wrapping paper, it is saying that our democracy is often just a sham, and that the problem is not so much spin as twist. It is a serious criticism of those who wield power - the subtle and not so subtle pressures they exercise - the patronage they use to get their way. It should be no surprise that lawyers, accountants, academics and others, from time to time compromise strict standards of professional behaviour and play word games instead. I have seen it happen. If the System does look itself in the mirror, it needs to recognise that the mirror itself is a distorting one. Will it do even that? Sad to say, the report has already been allowed to gather dust as reports of this kind invariably do, and everything goes on as before.

Like everyone else I have been an observer. What I have seen in one small part of Britain is, I suspect, a microcosm of the whole. What I have seen could happen anywhere, at any time. All of that is now ancient history for me. What I write here is fiction from first to last, but it is born of the experiences and of the paranoia of things that I have seen. And I write it as a tragedy, which I believe it is. I hope that I do not give too much away if I say that there are no individual heroes or heroines in the play, no individual villains either. All the characters are in one way or another victims or casualties of a system that has somehow lost its way. They're all human. If there is a hero, it is Brighouse School itself.

Thoughts about music, art, literature and God

All is not bad. There are opportunities as never before for those who can seize them. And pleasures abound for those who can afford them, or have been shown where to look for them. The world is a big and exciting place for those who can find their way around it. And as I have thought myself into the characters of Emma Kirk and John Errington, the Music and English teachers that I have created, both with a real sense of vocation, I have felt things about

Music and English that I was not aware of before. And I have thought more about God, especially in relation to the spiritual side of Music. I have been thinking about a Universal Creator through the prism of Music. They have, after all, been travelling companions since the dawn of civilisation.

Music is good for the soul. Whether playing or just listening, it is something you should learn at school. As Anthony Storr illustrated in his book *Music and the Mind* [11] it can have a special value for children with learning difficulties.[11] I am indebted to my music teacher who played records to us with, as I recall it, fibre tipped needles. Once learned at school, it will last a lifetime. It has for me. With great Music like great Art you can touch eternity. These are moments that will last for ever.

English, well English we take for granted, but we shouldn't. It is England's enormous gift to the world, enabling it to talk to itself. If offers its rich vocabulary and strange punctuation, which I can never seem to get absolutely right because I was never properly taught it in the first place. And it offers its great literature. - But then I am sure that the Romans didn't appreciate what a wonderful gift Latin of all languages was going to be to the world either.

What a legacy England has bequeathed with Shakespeare and Milton, with Wordsworth and Rupert Brooke, and with all the wonderful writers of today and yesterday. We have to make sure that their legacy is not lost along the way. Our schools also have to make sure that the children of those who have recently arrived at our shores are given every opportunity to see, hear, use and enjoy this legacy to the full. That is a major task in its own right, one of many they have, apart from meeting special educational needs.

And where does the inspiration come from for art, music and literature? Can it simply be explained by the laws of evolution? I'm not so sure. I shall return to this.

Thoughts about politics

For many years I went along with the idea, as I guess most people do, that 'Liberty, Equality and Fraternity' were, and are, worth going to the barricades for. But is it?

'Liberty', too often today confused with License, is in today's complex world constrained by rules and regulations. We are moving towards an

Orwellian State with cameras everywhere, computers that can read your every movement and censor your email, with DNA profiling and, as I write, with an ID card to come. This is a new world. Are you really free when you are intimidated, bullied or cajoled into doing things you shouldn't do or into not doing things you know you should? The play shows how easily this can happen today, and the consequences, when the abiding rule is ' to know your place'. But if Liberty is simply an absence of slavery or torture, is that really enough? It certainly was around the year 1800, but what about today?

'Equality' - who really does want Equality?[13] Only those painfully less equal or those who do not always practice what they preach. Not an argument for not wanting a fairer society, a fairer world and equality of opportunity. But 'Equality'? Is that the right word? Is it the right word in education? Is it the right word in health? Wouldn't the word 'Equity' be a far more realistic and an altogether better mantra? Deep down in Britain fairness and fair play are the words that really resonate, and make the country a good place to live in.

And 'Fraternity'? Some hope if you think about war and conflict over the years and to this day, right around the globe. Just how much 'fraternity' is there in our schools when, according to *Mencap*, eight out of ten children with learning disabilities are bullied, with some probably scarred for life?

In short, today Liberty is absolutely impossible to define. Equality is absolutely impossible to achieve, and Fraternity is simply impossible. What about Integrity, Diversity, Harmony, Accountability, and common decency? What about old fashioned Trust? None of these were ever listed. A bit of competence would help too, and a bit of wonder. We are driving blind. No wonder there are errors of judgment.

And here is another blind spot. Personal satisfaction sits alongside financial reward as a basic human need. That is why self-fulfilment and self esteem make a major contribution to personal happiness irrespective of income. Are they rated as important in the corridors of power? Specifically, are they rated as important in the Department for Education and Skills (DfES) and in Local Education Authorities (LEAs)? They should be. Life is not just about money and an opportunity to spend it. With today's excesses of drugs, drink, gambling and promiscuity, all increasingly off limit, happiness, especially in the young, is increasingly elusive. This should surprise no-one. It's what happens when you confuse liberty and licence, imagining that you are providing the one, when all you are doing is encouraging the other. It's what happens when pride is at a premium, when pills appear the best answer.

The highest common factor – Humanity?

In our troubled world we need an altogether new and simpler banner to say it all.

It should simply read 'Humanity'. In our newly discovered *global* world, this should now be the focal point of our aspirations, the spark to our idealism, the Litmus test for all human behaviour. It should be a marker post in the quest for peace, and against all forms of prejudice and discrimination.

Some people are there already - *Médecins Sans Frontières*[13] for instance and the thousands and thousands of people who do unsung, voluntary work quietly. There is also the army of those who care for their patients, or for their family, neighbours and friends. But still not nearly enough people rally behind the banner of 'Humanity', not least those best positioned to assert it in government, on a pulpit or in multinational companies. There its value is understated and at times undervalued in the pursuit of other things. Power over people can be a terrible responsibility. Shame on all those wielding it, and who abuse it!

Shouldn't we be defining what is humane and promoting it? Defining what is inhumane and condemning it? Shouldn't we try to identify who respects human life on this planet and who threatens it? Shouldn't we look within ourselves for compassion for those less fortunate than ourselves - children with special educational needs for example, and their parents? It is of the essence, yet sometimes we do these things, but sometimes we don't.

This does not divide people by race or by religion, by political persuasion or by gender. Yes, men and women are wired up differently, and one shouldn't assume otherwise, but they derive their energy from the same power source.

Asserting our common humanity distinguishes between fundamentalism that can be all right if it is simply a personal belief, but may well not be okay if it is fanatical, and impacts on those who do not share it. It distinguishes between dogma, which can also be all right, and bigotry which is not. It distinguishes between those who care about future generations on this planet and those who are motivated simply by avarice for money or for power or both. It divides between people who are basically humane and those who are basically inhumane. It's as simple as that. Sadly, not everyone that is human is humane.

And even in war, when the guns are firing, and when bombs and rockets are exploding, those who think that this has no relevance make a big mistake. Then it is just more difficult to define, and harder to achieve. The imperative however remains to help create the peace afterwards.

And we should stop thinking that when you are confronted by evil you have only a two-way choice, between appeasing it and confronting it. Appeasing it is an act of weakness that accepts it. Confronting it militarily can sometimes be an ultimate necessity, but sometimes is an act of lunacy, that feeds evil, by giving it the oxygen of publicity and a challenge that it actually relishes.

The third option is containment, an act of quiet strength. Quarantine the monster until it self destructs - until it dies of its own poison. We have seen this work with the rulers in the Kremlin and with Mao Tse Tung. Bad notions can no longer compete for long in our global world. Let them try, and then eventually fail. They will implode. Let people realise that just as Communism does not work, so other dogmas and ideologies have their fault lines too. That is how we should be dealing with religious fanaticism.

True faith and real doubt – room for both?

There is not much further to go now, as I share my thoughts with you. Stay with this just a little while longer! If I think about 'Humanity' I have been thinking too about God.[12] Religion and faith both come into the play. The music teacher in the play, Emma Kirk, is a Pentecostal Christian. She lives her faith, and she makes it her own. She breaks the rules and talks about it in the classroom. Terry, a pupil, expresses the doubts of his father, an atheist. Another parent, Ranjit Singh, a taxi driver is a Sikh. The English teacher, John Errington, is agnostic. The spirit of music carries a message to all of them.

I should tell you where I stand. I am a member of one of the smaller Jewish communities in the UK. I have an approach to my religion that is my own.

Along with about half of the world's population, I believe that there is a Creator. I sense that many, many people feel an enormous inborn need of a faith, a roadmap for this life and a passport to the next. At its best, for those who believe, faith is a wondrous gift from Heaven.

It explains the beginning and the end of existence. It helps people to live with themselves, and to seek forgiveness when they need it. With its ritual it provides constancy and a colour to communal identity. It is the source of solace and strength in the face of adversity; it provides a basis for compassion, reconciliation and healing, and it gives a set of values to live by. I think of people like Mother Teresa, Archbishop Desmond Tutu, Rev. Martin Luther King Jnr, Mahatma Ghandi and His Holiness the 14th Dalai Lama, Tenzin Gyatso. It is about birth, marriage and death, pain and guilt, and about loyalty to the tribe.

One of my closest friends is an atheist. That is his deeply held personal conviction, and there are many others who share it with him. He asserts that his values are at the very least as worthy as those founded upon a religious belief, and he reminds me of the blood that has been shed over the centuries, and to this day, with all the wild frenzy that comes only from religious fervour. As he is a retired senior officer from within the Fire Services, he must have a point.

And so I pose a question. With arrival on our shores of many representatives of the world's faiths, in what is a largely secular society, how are we all to live peaceably together on our small and crowded island? Why, in all humility, cannot mankind derive inspiration from the Prophets draw comfort not contention from the sacred word, and live together within the shared framework of the Laws of Noah?

The question starts in our schools. Emma Kirk, the music teacher in the play is simply happy in her faith. Why can't everyone else be happy in theirs? Can she talk about it in the classroom?

As one teacher put it to me when I asked her how she dealt with the very many faiths that are represented in her school in Leeds, she said "We celebrate everything". Many other teachers probably do the same. That must be much better than not celebrating anything, and much more likely to lead to social cohesion. And, why not some healthy scepticism too? All of this should not worry those who have true faith or real doubt. Sometimes political correctness may just occasionally not be correct.

A number of years ago I heard the following proposition which I endorse here. If there is one God, it shouldn't be outrageous to suggest that for the billions of people on this planet there are many paths to him or to her, just different routes up the same mountain, and that each one is equally valid and each one blessed. The Matterhorn above Zermatt in Switzerland looks quite unlike Monte Cervino in Italy, but it is the same mountain.

The strength of individual belief underpins the validity of one - it does *not* undermine the validity of another. It also underpins its integrity. No single way is exclusive, although Judaism, Christianity and Islam all find words to suggest that theirs is. If they have that belief, isn't it time for them to shed it? A compassionate God – or Allah the All-Merciful - in his wisdom must be allowed some continuing discretion as to whom he admits into his divine presence - now mustn't he?

I cannot believe that God has favourites among his children. There has been and still is too much suffering caused by those who have believed this. We are dealing here with the Infinite. There is no edge to the universe. The concept of God should reflect that. I am happy to echo here sentiments that others, much more learned than me, have expressed, most recently Chief Rabbi Sir Jonathan Sacks in his book, *The Dignity of Difference.*

God is not One but, if n stands for infinity, One to the power of n. That is a thought to unite all those who believe in a supreme deity. In the name of humanity they should rejoice in sharing it. The Alexandria Declaration of the three Faiths was a real start. It needs to continue.

Monotheism stems from tribes in the desert that couldn't live in harmony then any more than they would appear to be able to do so today. The Holy Land is an unholy mess. Jerusalem is not a city of peace. But those tribes produced Holy texts, the Torah, the Bible and the Koran. Beautiful documents. There is an exhibition of them in the British Library as I write. Incredible wisdom in their day, but both contain militant passages right for their day, but out of synch in our global world. They were written when the sun went round the earth, not the other way round, and when bullocks and goats were sacrificed upon an altar. They predate Copernicus, never mind the Hubble telescope and all the scientific discoveries of our times. Furthermore there are some things we are not given to know for sure or at all, and so many things scientists do not know even now.

So give Holy texts the respect they deserve, but not now an unquestioning literal obedience if that denies to God's presence compassion, and if it denies to people of other faiths or no faith at all their common humanity. We will need all the help Holy texts can give us if we are to contain HIV

Aids and confront the effects of climate change on our psyche, never mind on our landscape and on our financial resources.

So I say where I stand. We should see ourselves as partners on Planet Earth, not rivals, as bringing forth the blessing of tranquillity, not the curse of violence, and the gift of sacred beauty, not the ugly face of conflict. How can you educate a multi-ethnic society in any other way? People should not just come together in prayer only when they mourn their dead in war.

If writing this seems all a bit naïve, I still have a basic conviction in the worth of liberal values. That has nothing whatsoever to do with party politics. These values can be found sometimes, but sadly not always in most political parties. I hope that I am not too naïve asserting them here.

"Care, and take care" is the underlying message within the play. I am not sure that everyone does. Far too many people don't.

If not now, when?

We do need to take very great care of our heritage. Older civilisations than ours, from the East and from the West, respected their ancestors and the earth they came from. We should do the same. We need to reassert some of our own core values, and resurrect some time-hallowed norms. It is not critical whether they are based upon religious precept or simply upon rational judgment. And they are as much about our legacy to the generations to come, as to things we seek for ourselves, often in our own selfish interest.

How many natural or human disasters must take place, how many temples have to be destroyed, before we start to do this? See the final moments of the play in this context.

I toss this tiny pebble into a very large pond. I hope it may cause just a few ripples before it sinks to the bottom.

To close, a little story. Two seriously ill patients go to see a doctor. He examines the first. "Oh dear" he says, "I am most terribly sorry. I *cannot* do anything here." He then sees the second. "Oh dear, oh dear, oh dear. I *must* do something here." Hence a play within a book. Please see it with that in mind. See the whole as one picture, but see it as a fragment of a very large canvas.

DEATH OF A NIGHTINGALE

Programme Note

We shall not cease from exploration
And the end of all our exploring
Will be to arrive where we started
And know the place for the first time.

TS Eliot, Four Quartets, Little Gidding 1942

Inclusion – when did it all begin? On Monday, 7 October 1976, in a debate in the House of Lords on an Education Bill. That day a new clause, although criticised and withdrawn earlier in the year, was reintroduced in a slightly different form. It required Local Education Authorities to educate most children with special educational needs in mainstream schools instead of special schools.

At that time the policy had not been researched nor costed, and was opposed by many disability organisations and by the National Union of Teachers, but it nevertheless passed into law.

Since then the myth has been propagated that the Warnock Report issued two years later in 1978 shaped the policy of Inclusion. In fact a small unrepresentative pressure group, in a debate lasting no more than 41 minutes in the Upper House, had succeeded in pre-empting that report, and changed the face of special education for over thirty years.[2]

In 1994 the policy of Inclusion was reinforced by the Salamanca Conference organised by the Government of Spain and UNESCO which said amongst other things that *"those with special educational needs must have access to regular schools."* The educational establishment, supported by the Treasury, along with Academia then put its full weight behind it.

In 1988 Alan Share was invited to be a governor of Barbara Priestman, a school in Sunderland for physically disabled children. Shortly after that he was invited to serve as its chair of governors by the head teacher, and he remained on the governing body until 2004.

During this time he witnessed the efforts that were made by a local authority to close down what was widely acknowledged to be an excellent school in pursuit of the policy of Inclusion. By this time it had been endorsed by all three political parties and no-one in power then was questioning it.

These efforts, however, met with a campaign mounted by parents, staff and pupils, by the medical profession and by the wider community to keep the school open, a campaign that ultimately persuaded Charles Clarke, then Education Secretary, to veto the proposal to close it. The school is still open today.

However 100 special schools were closed during these years. To highlight the tragedy that he believes this to be, and to draw on his own experience of the benefits such schools can provide for their pupils, he brings Death of a Nightingale to the New End Theatre. The play, as it tells the fictional story of the efforts of Westborough's local authority to close Brighouse School, supports the argument that parents of children with special needs should be able to choose between mainstream and special schools for their children and that the scales should not be weighted against them.

We are delighted that Oak Lodge School, a special school in East Finchley, has helped to provide from its pupils the cast for a music lesson. Alan Share believes that music should be a part of every child's education. It had an important place at Barbara Priestman School and he accords it an important place at Brighouse School. He also uses it to explore the relationship between music and faith that have been bedfellows since the dawn of civilisation.[12]

In writing the music lesson, he draws on the Alexandria Declaration of 2002, which was issued by religious leaders from the Muslim, Christian and Jewish communities. This asserted: "*We seek to live together as neighbours respecting the integrity of each other's historical and religious inheritance.*" He also draws on Lord Sacks' recently published book The Dignity of Difference where he asserts that "*God is God of all humanity, but between Babel and the end of days no single faith is the faith of all humanity.*" He hopes the music that the music teacher Emma Kirk plays for her class will echo these sentiments. He also gives atheism and humanism their voice.

What he writes is fiction from first to last.

Alan Share sums it up in these words: "*The play is born of the experiences and of the paranoia of things that I have seen. I write it as a tragedy, which I believe it is.*

I hope that I do not give too much away if I say that there are no individual heroes or heroines in the play, and no individual villains either. All the characters are in one way or another victims or casualties of a system that has somehow lost its way. They are all human, and at the heart of the tragedy, is human frailty which always seems to bedevil the best of notions. If there is a hero, it is Brighouse School itself, and Tracy who tells its story. I have given her the last word, and it is right that she should have it."

*The British Journal of Development Disabilities Vol.52 Part 1 January 2006 No.102 pp 65-71.

DEATH OF A NIGHTINGALE
By Alan Share

CAST (in alphabetical order)

Shammi Aulakh	David Harding
	Ranjit Singh
Feyi Babalola	Emma Kirk
Cecila Delatori	Judy Fotheringham
	Eileen Winterton
	Judith Singh
	Wendy Robinson
Samantha Dorrance	Tracy
Jordan Loughran	Philippa
Peter Mair	James Harrington
Melanie Ramsay	Margaret Williamson
Ian Targett	John Errington
	Gerry Thompson

Also with the participation of pupils from the Oak Lodge School, East Finchley.

Romina Bemani-Naeini	Jean
James Le Dain	Henry
Max Lewis	Terry

CREW

Tom Scott	Director
Rachael Vaughan	Set & Costume
Aaron J Dootson	Lighting
Katy Munroe Farlie	Stage manager

ALAN SHARE

For over 17 years a governor of a special school in NE England, and chairman of governors for most of that time. He assisted its parents in their campaign to keep the school open.

Educated at Bede Grammar School, Sunderland and at Merton College, Oxford, after which he qualified as a barrister. Then a full, varied and interesting career before he retired, journeying from law to politics, and then to running a successful retailing company. He describes himself as a hybrid.

Taking a view that life was always most interesting on the margins, he was active in his trade association, notably chairing an industry wide action group that introduced Qualitas Conciliation Service in the furniture and carpet industry, now the Furniture Ombudsman.

He has been for many years chairman of a residential care home in Newcastle, chairman of the Newcastle branch of the National Association of Decorative and Fine Arts Societies, and a member of his local Rotary Club.

Travels widely, enjoys music, reading and the arts, and is never, ever bored.

His wife Ros also had an interest in helping the disabled. She assisted some of the pupils at the same special school with their reading. She also studied law at the then Newcastle Polytechnic, and used it to become a tribunal worker for a local CAB. Besides that she adjudicated at Social Security and Disability Appeal Tribunals in nearby towns.

You can visit www.deathofanightingale.com and read his Blog for other thoughts from the outside, looking in.

TOM SCOTT, THE DIRECTOR

Tom has directed over 100 productions including *The Widowing of Mrs Holroyd* and *The Lady From The Sea* at the New End Theatre.

Other London credits include *A Night in November* (Etcetera Theatre and UK Tour). He was Artistic Director of Eye Theatre, Suffolk where his favorite productions included *Oleanna, Speed the Plow, Shrivings, An Inspector Calls, As You Like It, The Taming of the Shrew, The Norman Conquests, Miss Julie, Love Child, Pygmalion* and *Hedda Gabler.*

He has now established Eye Theatre Company to present London-based productions and national tours.

SHAMMI AULAKH

Shammi was born in West London. He studied Acting at the London Academy of Performing Arts for two years. Theatre credits include *Bina's Choice* (Dominion Centre) *Survivors* (Orange Tree Theatre) *Papa Was a Bus Conductor* (Edinburgh Fringe) *Deranged Marriage* (Rifco Arts) *Across the Black Waters* (Man Mela Theatre) *Marriage of Figaro* (Tara Arts) *Balti King, Ghost Dancing, Fourteen Songs Two Weddings and a Funeral, Sweet Cider & Wuthering Heights* (Tamasha Theatre Company). He has done numerous corporate training videos. TV & Commercial Credits: *MFI, Kodak, FT, Aerial, BT, Operation X, Days That Shook The World* Film Credits : *Hypnotic* (Kismet Films) *Friday* (Academy Films) *Goal II* (Goal Prods Ltd) *Saxon* (Sillwood Films).

Shammi is also a Filmmaker. His first film *The Fourteenth* was set during World War II. His second film *Frozen Bamboo* is currently in post production and will be shown at the Midnight Sun Film festival in Finland. He is currently working on a script called *Liberty.*

FEYI BABALOLA

Feyi Babalola trained at the Identity Drama School. TV credits include Shoot *The Messenger* (BBC), *Dick and Dom's in Da Bungalow* (BBC), *The Friday Night Project* (C4) and feature film *Love And Other Disasters* (Skyline Films).

Feyi also wrote and starred in the critically acclaimed, award winning play *Southern Blues.*

CECILIA DELATORI

Cecilia is an award winning writer/performer. Her credits include Fringe First winning one-woman show *Tonight I'm Entertaining Richard Gere* which was also nominated for a London Fringe award. Her current *Sparkling one-woman comedy* (WhatsOnStage.com) *Beyonce, Stop Punching Robbie!* premiered with great success at The Gilded Balloon and then at Leicester Square Theatre. *Spectacles, Bibles, Inflatable Bras* also a one-woman show premiered at The Pleasance, Edinburgh and subsequent sell out success on tour.

Theatre credits include Madam Arcati in *Blithe Spirit*, the nurse in *Romeo and Juliet* and Mrs Pearce in *Pygmalion* at The Eye Theatre. Also, *Lady Macbeth Firmed my Buttocks* and comedy sketches for the TBA Comedy Sketch Club at The Gate, Notting Hill. Radio credits: *Teresa* for the *Inner Voices* series on BBC Radio 4 and a Radio commercial for Coca Cola. She has also played in *Without Motive* (ITV).

Cecilia is also a stand up musical comedian and will be performing at the Edinburgh Festival Fringe this year.

SAMANTHA DORRANCE

Actress, Singer, Dancer and TV Presenter Samantha Dorrance has been working in theatre and television since the age of 2. Since then she has gone onto working in many TV and Theatre Productions including such TV programs as *Midsomer Murders*, *Hollyoaks* and many projects with Disney Channel UK and USA - working with such well known actors as Zac Efron.

Samantha has also had extensive experience within Theatre and Pantomime. She has recently played Margot in *And this was Odd* and appeared in a number of productions at the Theatre Severn in Shrewsbury, playing such roles as Wendy in *Peter Pan* and the title Role in *Cinderella*.

Off the screen and stage, Samantha enjoys being creative. She is currently studying music at college, plays a variety of instruments and enjoys writing and recording her own music in her spare time.

JORDAN LOUGHRAN

Jordan is a very young and talented actress.

She recently played in *Spur of the Moment* at the Royal Court, but she also appeared in TV productions such as *UGetMe* and *Saving Nellie* and presented *Richmond English 24.*

Jordan's work also includes a radio participation in *The Lamplighter.*

She is currently studying Languages at University.

PETER MAIR

Graduating from RADA in 1964, Peter worked in rep, on TV and with the RSC until 1967. Peter then switched to theatre administration, working *inter alia* for eighteen years as Drama officer for the Arts council of Great Britain, until 1988. Peter returned to professional acting in 1989, since when theatre has included, *The Taming of the shrew* (Cambridge Theatre Co), *Sir Courtly Nice* (Magnificent Theatre Company), *The Sound of Music* (two national tours), *The Applecart* (Ipswich Wolsey), *Statues of Liberty* (Very Fine Productions at New End Theatre), *The school for Scandal* (English Touring Theatre), *All My Sons* (Basingstoke Haymarket), *Othello* (Talawa Theatre Co), *Carousel* (National Tour), *Jack & the Beanstalk* (Salisbury Playhouse), *Krapp's Last Tape* (Bright Blue Productions), *Oliver!* (Aberystwyth Arts Centre), *City of Angels* (English Theatre Frankfurt), *Darling Buds of May - Perfick* (Groundlings Theatre Co), *The Importance of Being Earnest* (Antic Disposition), *Tosca* (Royal opera House), *The Beautiful Couple and The Big A* (SWWJ), *Visiting Frank* (Lost Theatre Short Play Festival at New End Theatre), *Tristan and Isolde* (Royal Opera House).

Television has included London's Burning, The Bill, Eastenders, Broolrside, The Courtroom, Into the Fire, Ruth Rendell Mysteries, Chucklevision. Radio has included *Mothers of Invention,* The Great Smog, The Fast Girl, all Pier Productions for BBC R4.

Films have included *Being Human* (Enigma Films), *Ernest* (John McKenzie Productions), *David* (Lube srl for Turner Television). Peter has appeared in TV commercials for the UK, the USA, Denmark, Ireland, Spain and Switzerland. Peter is an experienced voice over and role player.

MELANIE RAMSAY

Melanie trained at the Guildhall School of Music and Drama.

Theatre credits include: *Red Black and Ignorant* (Cock Tavern Theatre), *No, Not, Not,Not,Not Enough Oxygen* (Cockpit Theatre), *So Long Life* (Theatre Royal, Bath), *Mr. Colport* (Royal Court), *Martha, Josie and Chinese Elvis* (Bolton Octogon),*An Ideal Husband* (Theatre Royal Haymarket), *Saved* (Bolton Octogon),*Communicating Doors* (Manchester Library),*As you like it* (Colchester Mercury), *Northanger Abbey* (Colchester Mercury), *The Importance of Being Earnest* Royal Exchange, *Time of My Life* (Manchester, Library), *Bare* (Oldham, Coliseum), *A Patriot for Me* (Royal Shakespeare Company).

Film credits include *On Your Own* (DDFilms), *Stoned* (Wild and Wicked Ltd.),*Come Together* (Working Titale TV), *Hamlet* (Fishmonger Films), *Midnight Movie* (Whistling Gypsy Productions),*The Crane* (BFI Films), *Upstairs* (Film Short).

Melanie has also appeared in several BBC TV Productions: *Holby City, Doctors,Casualty, House of Eliott.* TV credits also include *Talk to Me* (Company Productions), *Bad Girls* (Shed Prods), *No Child of Mine* (Meridian), *A Touch of Frost* (YTV), *The Rector's Wife* (Talisman), *The Bill* (Thames),

Commercials include: *Oatbix, Chelsea BS, Autoglass,Fox's Biscuits, Aral, Tesco.*

IAN TARGETT

Ian trained at RADA. Theatre credits include *Bows and Arrows* (Royal Court), *Why Me* (Strand), *The Kiss of Life* and *A View of Kabul* (Bush Theatre), *Romeo and Juliet* (Lyric, Hammersmith), *Beached* (Warehouse and Old Red Lion), *Eurydice* (Battersea Arts Centre), *Burning Point* (Tricycle), *The Woman In Black* (PW Productions), Absent Friends (Watford), *Waiting for Godot* (Oxford Playhouse), *Loot*, *The Tenant of Wildfell Hall*, *Absurd Person Singular*, and *Season's Greetings* (Birmingham Rep), *A Small Family Business* (West Yorkshire Playhouse), *Stars and Strive* (Crucible, Sheffield), *Tartuffe* (Theatr Clwyd), *Time and Time Again*, *See How They Run*, *Donkey's Years*, and *A Touch of the Sun* (Salisbury Playhouse), *Turn of the Screw* a two hander (Coliseum, Oldham) *Candida* (Bolton), *And a Nightingale Sang* (Southampton) *Moving Susan*, *Corpse* and *A Christmas Carol* (Basingstoke). *Just Between Ourselves* (Exeter) *Out of Order*, *One for the Road*, and *Confusions* (Sonning) National tours include *An Inspector Calls*, *The Winslow Boy* and *Arsenic and Old Lace*.

Television credits include Leslie in *Marks* by Alan Bennett, Geoff in *A Taste of Honey*, Spence in *Over the Rainbow*, DS Ball in *Mind Games* by Linda La Plante, Lind in *The Last Detective*, Captain Lyle in *Ghostboat*, Steve Dove in *Midsomer Murders, Trust Me, Casualty, Forever Green, Doctors, Bad Boys, Law and Disorder, The Fugitive, Bust* and *Grange Hill*.

On film Ian has appeared in *The Fool, A Dangerous Man, The Lover* and *The Spell*.

His many radio plays and series' include *Henry V, Rat in the Skull, The Aquarium of Coincidences, Monkshood* and *Second Thoughts*.

AARON J DOOTSON

Aaron graduated from Wimbledon College of Art in 2009 where he studied Lighting Design and Practice qualifying with a distinction. Aaron is a freelancing lighting designer specialising in theatre and based mainly in London.

Theatre credits include: *Tipping Point* – Bristol Hamilton House/ New Wimbledon Studio, *Bluebird* – Cockpit Theatre, *This Is How It Goes* – Kings Head Theatre, *Siren* – Etcetera Theatre, *Leo You Nutter* – Wimbledon College of Art, *Tape* – North Outlet Theatre Company

Dance credits include: *Mitosis Cloning* – Peacock Theatre, *Radical* – Sadlers Wells Theatre, *Extract* – Salders Wells Theatre, *Smash* – Sadlers Wells Theatre, and *Strangers* – Stratford Circus. All for Impact Dance.

As an assistant lighting designer: *Never Forget* (Uk Tour 2009 - LD James Whiteside).

Current relights: *Private Peaceful* (Uk Tour 2011 – LD Wayne Dowdeswell).

His website is aaronjdootson.co.uk.

RACHAEL VAUGHAN

Rachael Vaughan is a Central School of Speech and Drama graduate in Design for Performance 2010. Trained in all aspects of Set, Media and Costume Design, she has enjoyed working with a variety of directors and theatrical companies across London and the Southern U.K. These include James Purefoy, Fanshen Theatre, Grainne Byrne of Scarlett Theatre and Jon Wright of Tressel Theatre company.

Her recent and upcoming credits include, *74 Georgia Avenue* and *Death of a Nightingale* at The New End Theatre, Hampstead. *Fragments 2* at The Riverside Studios, Hammersmith. *Lyric Lounge Artist* in Residence for the Youth Theatre program, Studio One. *The Captive* by Ben Ellis, at The Stage's Top Fringe 100 venue 2010, The Finborough Theatre. *Lesbian BathHouse* at Edinburgh Fringe Festival's Assembly Rooms, George Street and she has a continued association with Equal Measure Production Company.

Rachael, originally from Bristol, also has significant training in Modern Dance, Classical music and Production photography which has enabled her to work at The Trinity Laban Conservatoire of Opera and produce work as an artist in her own right.

*Music in the background –
Ladysmith Black Mambazo –
"Music knows no Boundaries".
Tracy is in a wheel chair.*

ACT ONE

PREAMBLE

TRACY Hi, my name is Tracy. My friends call me Katy, Katy. You see I had a dream. I wanted to become an actress. I love the theatre. Kate Winslett, yes Titanic. I dreamt this dream at Brighouse School. I started there when I was four. It helped to make me who I am. It was my "hero". What happened to my school is what the play's about.

We had lots of fun. I bet other schools don't have wheelchair races. We even had a swimming pool, I call it our duck pond. Most of my pals had health problems, cerebral palsy like Pete, or spina bifida like Jesse, or cystic fibrosis like me. – you need a medical dictionary here. All sorts of things - speech problems, Crohn's, brittle bones. My friend Tommy Dixon died. He was only thirteen. All the school went into mourning when he died. It was so sad.

Some people didn't like an all age school, but it worked. Let me tell you about the people I loved. Our school nurse, Babs, she was always kept pretty busy. Our physio, Bunty. She massaged my legs between lessons. It was lovely. Some of my friends got help with speech and language. John Errington. He taught me English. He gave me my love of drama. Took me to the RSC. That's what gave me my dream of going on the stage. And I love singing. I sang *Annie*. You know "Tomorrow, Tomorrow, I love you Tomorrow." That's why I liked our music lessons. We had a wonderful teacher, Emma, Caribbean sunshine. I nearly forgot, our head teacher, Margaret Williamson. In my diary I call her Mummy Margaret. You see we were one great big family. Our motto was "All for One". She really cared about each one of us. I loved our ethos … when John explained to me what the word meant.

All sorts of people gave their time to the school, especially our mums and dads. They campaigned to keep the school open.

I was in Wesborough's Amateur Dramatics. John Errington encouraged me to join. I thought they wouldn't want me. And I must mention our band, our fantastic steel drum band. I played in it. We seemed to be performing somewhere every other week.

Despite all this, some people wanted to close us down. They thought we should all go to mainstream schools. I wanted to stay at Brighouse. Our mums and dads asked me to help their campaign to keep the school open. I even went on the telly. I did. Those people thought they were helping us, putting us in mainstream schools. I often used to wonder whether they really understood what it was like to have serious health problems and not find learning easy on top of that? And did they begin to understand what it's like to be bullied on top of everything else?

Did they? Most kids like us are for ever being bullied in mainstream schools. Did they know? And did they know what it was like for their mums too, when they came back home? I know what it's like. I saw "fluff" my pussy cat after a little boy tossed a bucket of water over her for a bit of fun. Did they know about all the other quite different special needs?

I'll tell you something. Lawyers and politicians just love to give us our rights. Rights. I call them buttercups and daises. And we are those little white dandelion heads, you know, they blow away in the wind.

Scene 1

Head teacher's living room
The room is dimly lit. Margaret Williamson is stretched out on couch, her arm touching the floor. She is semi-comatose. A glass and an empty bottle are beside her. John Errington lets himself in, but leaves the door ajar. He switches on the light. He suddenly sees Margaret. He thinks she is dead. He immediately thinks that Margaret has taken overdose. He thinks that he may have himself have contributed to this by walking out. He may even have been a bit selfish in arguing with her.

JOHN (Crying *and shaking Margaret*) Oh my God, pussy cat, what have you done. (*picks up 'phone*) .... Ambulance quickly ....John Errington ... I'm t 12 Oakley Way, Westborough, ... I think it's W13 5 NX...(*dashes back to Margaret*) Sweetie, wake up. Wake up. *(Back to the phone)* Sorry 07524 39102 ... A lady here ... Margaret Williamson ... seems to have taken an overdose ... please come as quickly as you can. I must try and wake her. (*Back to Margaret*) Oh my God, don't go (*back to the 'phone*) .... Yes ... she's still breathing but I can't wake her. ... Oh No. Oh. I think she's gone. Oh No. Margie without you. Wake up. The School. Our lovely kids. Us. Pussy cat, wake up. Oh God, Please, please not goodbye. Do wake up. A ship without a rudder. That's what we'll Yes. Oh God she left me a note (*Sees last line. Crumples it into his pocket*). Oh.No. Oh God. (*sobbing*) Ah. What about us? Didn't you care about us? Didn't you? (*Ambulance men enter – John leaves his house key on the table*) Oh, you silly little pussy cat.

Scene 2

TRACY Mummy Margaret didn't deserve it. She really didn't. Where do I start? I'd love you to see what some of our lessons were like.

Music room
Spring 2002. The Music Room of Brighouse School is set out with guitars and other instruments around the wall. There is also a TV, CD/DVD and speakers. Looking through the window, it is summer.

Five pupils are practicing on steel drums for a local gig. Emma Kirk is sitting at an upright piano, shows them calypso rhythm.

EMMA Jean, to end this lesson lead us in with a calypso. You know whenever I hear a calypso I hear the sweet voice of Harry Belafonte singing it on his imaginary island in my homeland, in the Caribbean.

JEAN Isn't this your homeland now?

EMMA This is my homeland too. You can have two passports. You can have two homelands. I am twice blessed. Actually I'm three times blessed. God is also my homeland. I am just so sorry for those poor folk who don't have any at all.

TRACY Do you still think about the country where your family came from?

EMMA Sure I do. And I know what my folk must have felt when they came here.

JEAN What?

EMMA Wow, this country's wet and grey. Jamaica, oh fo' Jamaica, where the sun shines all day... and folk drink rum and sing and dance all night long. That's where our rhythm comes from. Our rum. Come on let's have some rhythm in our music this morning. Imagine you're Trinidadians beating it out on their oil drums.

They start playing "Island in the Sun".

Scene 3

In the head teacher's room. Margaret Williamson has been joined by Ranjit and Judith Singh. Emma Kirk and Tracy knock and enter.

MARGARET Harry'll be fine while we talk. Wendy's wonderful with kids. She'll show her around the place. Emma, so pleased you can join us. Come on in. Tracy, thank you for coming too. This is Mr. & Mrs. Singh. I'm hoping that their son Harry will be joining us next term. Emma and the school band are our best ambassadors. Thought you should meet them.

EMMA You know, music's for our kids like God's gift of leaven is to bread.

MARGARET Mr. Singh knows us. His taxi ferries kids here. EMMA I thought I recognised you.

MARGARET Harry's had real bad luck. You have only to look at his bones and they break.

JUDITH He'd just mended his leg - broke it when a bully tripped his up on the stairs -and now he's broken her arm, slipped on some chewing gum.

RANJIT I'm afraid he's an accident waiting to happen. Kids tease him like mad. Say he's always "plastered."

EMMA He won't get teased here. Not so long as she lets us all autograph his plaster.

JUDITH Will Harry be able to join the band?

EMMA Not if he's got that plaster on. You know our Band won a Cup in the National Schools Band Competition. With a bit of luck he'll be able to join us when we defend our title next year.

MARGARET Tracy, you know more about the school than I do. Tell the Singh's what it's like for you. You were only four when you joined us weren't you?

TRACY Yes I was, and I can still remember feeling very lost when I came. I love it now.

MARGARET We've got a highly skilled team here. They put in the groundwork in the early years. A lot of nurturing goes on then. It bears fruit later on. Look at Tracy's progress, and you'll see what I mean. She is doing really well.

EMMA That's very true. Kids start believin' in themselves. Then it's safe for them to go in the big wide world. That's where Inclusion really matters, isn't it?

MARGARET You see the young kids are helped all along the way, seeing what the older ones can do, being encouraged by them. The older ones say things we can't.

EMMA You see it happening in the playground all the time, or when they help wheel each other around. Very little bullying goes on here.

RANJIT You're dead right. I've seen how they all get on together on the school run.

MARGARET My philosophy is that there's nothing our kids can't do that mainstream kids can. We had some out abseiling just last week. Do you think Harry would like to try?

RANJIT He'd be frightened to.

JUDITH He'd be frightened. I'd be terrified.

MARGARET Don't worry, we won't force our kids to do anything they don't want to do.

EMMA Wasn't it Helen Keller, blind and deaf from a baby, who said "Security is an illusion. Life is either a daring adventure or it is nothing at all."

MARGARET True. We don't mollycoddle our kids, Emma, but we won't push our luck either... It's amazing though what some of our kids do. There's little John Turnbull. He controls his wheelchair and his computer with a wand attached to his forehead.

EMMA He is just so bright.

MARGARET His mum was really chuffed to see his progress when she came in yesterday. He's such a happy little boy.

EMMA Such a lovely smile.

MARGARET We've had to give him a lot of time. I must tell you about Tracy's great claim to fame. (*Tracy holds her head in her hands with shame at the memory*) At one of our Presentation evenings - you know we have lots of fun and entertainment as well as prize giving on these great occasions - well, she caught my predecessor full in the face with a custard pie... she was supposed to miss.

TRACY He was supposed to duck. I paid the price the following year. I was asked to be Jack in the Box. I was inside that box for ages. He said he forgot I was there. Do you believe that?

MARGARET Do you believe anything in this world Tracy? That's one of the lessons we teach you. Another is that everyone can achieve something in life with a helping hand. They don't always find it in mainstream schools.

TRACY Jean was locked in a cupboard once in her old school. Some classmates they were. The cleaners let her out.

MARGARET Jean had a hard time. Her pals kept ribbing her, calling her "spacker". Her mum took her away from school. It was so bad. Finally came here. You wouldn't believe it. She wants to be a journalist. She runs the school newspaper, and the local paper has had her in the newsroom. In this school we believe that kids are capable of anything.

RANJIT I can believe that. Do you know about Fred Raffle? He's blind. You know he played cricket with dried peas inside the ball so you could hear it. A suitcase was the wicket.

TRACY Wow

RANJIT Yes, it's true. He was mad keen on cricket. He worked out how he could play the game with his pals at a school for the blind. And my goodness, he now commentates on international cricket. You know, I heard him commentate when India played England. There's guts for you.

MARGARET Fantastic. That's exactly what we find here, and what we encourage. I hope mainstream schools find the time to do the same. The trouble is I don't think they always do, and certainly teaching assistants are not always trained to stretch kids. You need years of training and experience for that. But that's by the way. Tracy, tell the Singh's about our Paralympians.

TRACY Philippa and Gordon Davis competed in the Athens Paralympics. Philippa won a Silver in the wheelchair 800 metres and Gordon won a Gold in the 4 x 400 relay.

MARGARET We had a team of three out there. Gordon Davis did fantastically well.

RANJIT Do they still want to close this School down?

EMMA Look guys, do you still need us?

MARGARET Yes, you two can leave us now. Don't let me keep you, Tracy.

RANJIT I've so enjoyed meeting you, and (*turning to Tracy*) you, too.

(*Emma and Tracy leave the room*)

RANJIT What is going to happen to this school? I don't want Harry to come here if they are going to close it.

JUDITH The LEA said it could happen.

MARGARET They certainly did want to, until our parents persuaded them not to. It was some campaign. They didn't know what hit them.

JUDITH I read all about it in the local papers.

MARGARET Well, they had been warned. They held a meeting at the school and tried to sell mainstream schools to our parents. The parents asked for a vote at the end of the meeting, and all the parents, every single one of them, put up their hands saying that they didn't agree. But, of course, they just went ahead.

RANJIT I thought they were supposed to listen to parents.

MARGARET Well you read what happened in the press. The Minister stopped the closure plan.

RANJIT So how does it stand now?

MARGARET As I said, the Minister threw out the closure plan. You know, if ever they close this school it will break my heart. If they close us down, it will be over my dead body.

Scene 4

Left Stage

TRACY Unfortunately there were people who wanted to do just that. At about the same time we were having our music lesson, four of them were meeting up at the regional office of the Department for Education and Skills. I call them the execution squad. They thought that they were right. A lot of people did, and probably still do.

Regional office, DfES – managing Inclusion
There is a desk and a round table and 4 chairs. On the desk there is a photograph of Rebecca, Judy Fotheringham's daughter. Regional officer Judy Fotheringham is first joined by a civil servant from London, James Harrington, and then by the Director of Education, David Harding, and head of Special Needs, Gerry Thompson from Westborough City Council. After introductions and pleasantries, they discuss the closure of Brighouse School. It has been thwarted by a strong campaign by parents to keep it open. Over 15,000 reasoned objections persuaded the Minister to reject plan to close the school.

JUDY *(on the telephone)* Yes, I did listen to the repeat of "Yes Minister". I do admire Sir Humphrey.

James Harrington knocks and enters

JAMES Are you talking about me?

JUDY (*still on the 'phone*) God has just walked in. I'll ring you back later. Bye (*To James*) Hello, good to see you again.

JAMES Nobody's ever said I had a divine presence before. Mind you they thought my father had when he was a District Commissioner in the Punjab. But people do turn to me for the occasional miracle.

David Harding and Gerry Thompson knock and enter.

DAVID I hope we're not interrupting.

JAMES Come in

DAVID Sorry we're a bit late. Can I introduce Gerry Thompson? He heads up our Inclusion team. You've met already haven't you, Judy?

JUDY Yes, last autumn.

JAMES We haven't had the pleasure. I'm so glad you've come. Do you mind if we get down to business straightaway? Yes?

(*They all settle round James*).

JAMES Thank you, Judy, for setting up this meeting. The Minister suggested that I see you. He does think that this situation needs to be actively managed. He didn't like having to reject your proposals, David, but he really had no alternative. DAVID I agree. I don't hold it against him.

JAMES And we don't hold it against you. But we certainly don't want other parents copying them. Fifteen and half thousand objections giving reasons why the school should not be closed, and two TV celebrities and a former international footballer.

GERRY We can do without that again.

JAMES Yes, We don't mind petition signatures. There can be millions of them so far as we are concerned. Ultimately we just shred them and recycle the paper. It's a great safety valve for the disgruntled. Objections with reasons - that's another matter. Each one of them is shred resistant.

DAVID You're dead right, but our political masters say that we have to consult.

GERRY They just don't realise how much time it wastes when parents take the offer seriously.

JAMES That's one of the things that the Department is worried about. We just don't want it to catch on. This is the second time it's happened. It's getting to be a habit - one we can do without. We've now taken the Minister out of the firing line here and set up School Organisation Committees to deal with school closures. They can take the flak.

GERRY A really clever move, a gesture to local democracy. Makes it much easier for us to deal with.

JAMES But we still don't want the idea to catch on.

JUDY I did have a word with David about that.

DAVID Yes and I had a word with the Head. She understood.

JAMES Good. That's one of the things the Minister was very worried about. The other, of course, is how you get the show back on the road. We need that. Some people in the disability organisations have been pushing for this for over thirty years.

DAVID I thought Warnock started it in '78.

JAMES No, she put the icing on the cake. What provoked it was bad experiences some people had of special schools, parents as well as kids well before that.

JUDY Real dead end places, out of sight out of mind.

DAVID People like Lord Rix and David Blunkett hated young kids being segregated.

JAMES I've met them both. They'd both had bitter experiences. Did you know? I was at the UNESCO conference at Salamanca in ninety four. Nearly a hundred countries all saying that children with special needs had a right to mainstream education.

GERRY I wish I'd been there.

JAMES Well that certainly galvanised us into action. I've never seen Parliament move so fast, and so decisively. Don't think that the Minister doesn't realise that change can be a bit painful. He knows that in every good parent there is a Luddite trying to get out.

GERRY We've got a few of them at Brighouse.

JAMES It's your job Gerry to illuminate them, to show them the way to truth and light. You just have to. You see the Treasury has made up its mind that there are savings to be made here if they invest in it. You know the figures. Three per cent of children have special needs but they gobble up eight per cent of the total spend on education. That really isn't equitable.

DAVID Between these four walls I don't think Inclusion is going to be a cheap option.

JAMES Well, leading accountants advised us that we could make some real savings simply by reducing the number of Statements LEAs have to write for children with special needs.

DAVID We'll see.

GERRY And writing Statements is a real headache.

JAMES We'll have to keep some schools for kids with profound difficulties or very complex behavioural problems, but most can go.

JUDY I'm sure you're right.

JAMES And that brings us back to Brighouse School and its wingeing parents. What are you going to do?

JUDY I thought we could suggest to the Local Council that they bring in a consultant, you know one who would say the right thing, get his recommendations and put them to the School Organisation Committee. Of course, he'd consult first.

JAMES I am not sure that that is the best answer. You have got to win over the parents. They have a bird in their hands, and they like it. We are offering them, as they see it, two in the bush. Where are they going to get their next dinner from? Not from the bush unless we make their bird look a bit less appetising.

DAVID Well what are you actually proposing, James?

JAMES I am not proposing anything.

DAVID Suggesting, then.

JAMES I'm not suggesting anything either. This is a journey of exploration.

DAVID Or a safari where the wild beasts roam.

GERRY And vultures fly overhead ready to scavenge their next meal.

DAVID I've seen them. They're the parents of Brighouse School.

JAMES Look, it's up to you how you manage this. It'll be unpleasant, but really run the school down. When you finally deliver the message that the School has to close there'll be no great argument.

DAVID I hope you're right. There's a lot of support for the school in Westborough. Have you seen the local press? The Gazette's really anti. They've certainly had a good war.

GERRY I'm sure we can turn that around.

JAMES Exactly. Pharaoh wasn't put off his grand design for the Pyramids by carping criticism in the Alexandria Times.

DAVID One difference. I'm not Pharaoh. The Leader of the Council is, and he's afraid of losing his seat. Look, it'll actually run itself down in time, as we admit fewer kids to it. Some redundancies will be unavoidable and they won't be able to deliver the national curriculum.

GERRY The bird's already beginning to look a bit sick. Their roll came down last year by nine pupils.

JAMES The key is to get the Head teacher on side. You really must try to do that.

GERRY To get the egg to accept the frying pan. You're right there.

DAVID Easier said than done. I know Margaret Williamson. You don't.

JAMES She must know that virtue has its own reward, but there'll be nothing for her if she's awkward. She will need another school when the School is closed. You do write her references, after all.

DAVID Yes, we do. But that's a trade secret. Governors might do it more knowledgeably, maybe more honestly. We do it more... er purposefully. Okay. I guess you're both right. I'll go along with it.

JAMES Look, I don't want to be involved in the fine details of all this. But do keep me informed and we'll watch your backs for you. OFSTED won't cause you any trouble.

JUDY Can we all meet again to progress this?

JAMES I don't think we need a minute of this meeting.

DAVID Could you drop me a note just confirming that it has taken place? It will help with the Leader, too. He's not a happy Pharaoh at the moment.

JAMES I'll send you something suitable, a comfort letter if that is what you'd like. It won't be very explicit. Don't worry about the ten plagues. They don't apply to us. Purges very, very occasionally. Plagues, never.

DAVID That's okay.

JAMES You are a cautious bastard.

DAVID Bastard today, war wounded tomorrow unless I am careful.

JAMES Oh, by the way, the Treasury has agreed to cough up some more grant aid for those authorities able to progress Inclusion.

DAVID I had already heard that.

JAMES We do everything we can to help. I must be off. There's a train at noon. Can you get me to the Station?

JUDY Ask Susan next door. She'll book a taxi for you.

JAMES Will do. A very good use of time today. Thanks again for everything ... and good luck.

(*James Harrington leaves the room*)

DAVID (*with a smile*) You know, James Harrington is a total wanker. I bet he'll get home tonight to game pie washed down with a fine bottle of vintage wine.

JUDY He deserves it.

GERRY Well, for me it'll be pork pie washed down with Chateau plonk. That'll do me just nicely.

DAVID Tell me; is that a photo of your daughter?

JUDY Yes, Rebecca. I'm putting her through university.

DAVID What's she studying?

JUDY Bio-engineering. A chip off the other old block. Her father was a lecturer in chemistry. He passed away, last year. Prostate cancer. Took him early. He didn't have a PSA test until too late.

DAVID I'm sorry. I didn't know. It must have been difficult.

JUDY It was, but the job helped, and it's so much more important to me now. Of course I've got Rebecca. She's been wonderful, but she's left the nest.

DAVID Bio engineering must be better than social engineering.

JUDY A bit more ambitious. Helping the Planet and all that.

GERRY Good on her.

JUDY Anyway, we've still got to deal with our little patch of it.

DAVID You're right. We've got a little engineering of our own to do, haven't we? I don't think that there's anything more to discuss at this time.

JUDY No, it's over to you now.

DAVID Gerry?

GERRY No, I think that's everything.

(*David Harding and Gerry Thompson leave to go.*)

JUDY And let's keep it that way. Keep in touch. By the way, there's a speed trap on North Road just past the Golden Lion. You need to watch for it.

DAVID Thanks for that. I do try to be a law-abiding citizen. Bye

GERRY Bye.

(*Exit David and Gerry*)

Scene 5

Left Stage

TRACY Let's get back to Brighouse School, shall we? You'll remember that Mummy Margaret said she liked to stretch us. She said that some of us even went abseiling. Well, I was one of them. I was so scared at the time. I had butterflies in my tummy the size of pomegranates. Jean told me to sing on the way down. Tomorrow, Tomorrow, Tomorrow. And all my pals cried out Katy, Katy, Katy. Well, I'll tell you something. Next summer I'm going paragliding in Wales. Anyway, they stretched us, but we stretched them. I haven't mentioned our carer Wendy. We called her Poo Bah. You see she took some of us to the loo. We were sometimes closer to her than to our teachers. So, come into the staff room and meet her and some of the others.

Staff Room – a mood of unease

There are comfortable chairs around the room. A coffee machine is in one corner. It is shortly after 4pm. John Errington, Emma Kirk and Wendy Robinson are relaxing.

Margaret storms in.

MARGARET God, that Terry James is impossible. How can you teach a class with him in it?

EMMA What's he been up to now?

MARGARET I asked him to describe an earthquake. Do you know what he said? "When my dad came home drunk." I then made a big mistake. I asked him what a volcano was then. And he said "My Mam, when my dad came home drunk".

WENDY It's not a joke. Have you seen his dad? He must be all of 20 stone.

MARGARET Mostly beer

WENDY If there's an earthquake in that family it'll be all of seven on the Richter scale. He's great when he is sober. Life and soul of the party. When he's had too many, he is the party.

MARGARET And you've seen his mum. When she blows her top, talk of molten lava. But he's still a terrible handful in class.

WENDY Isn't he just a naughty kid? I know more about him than you do. When you toilet kids they talk to you, and Terry talks to me more than he talks to you. I mean really talks. You know his home must be bedlam. I don't think his mother can cope.

MARGARET Neither can I. He's a bundle of mischief whatever the cause.

EMMA Same in my book, I'm afraid.. I've got everyone singing DO RE ME and he goes ME RE DO.

MARGARET And he shouts. And never sits still for a moment.

WENDY Well, I do have to toilet him more than any other kid in the school. I don't know where he gets it all from.

MARGARET He's probably a secret beer drinker - he'll take after his father mark my words - beer's a diuretic you know. Anyway I had a word with nurse about him. She thinks he's a candidate for Ritalin.

EMMA There's far too many kids on that these days. It's getting like chewing gum.

MARGARET Sorry to interrupt you. We're supposed to be having a staff meeting tomorrow. I thought we could make it a little training session instead. Yes?

(Everyone nods in agreement.)

MARGARET Okay. Can we focus on getting our kids going, really going? We know they have a lot of anger, a lot of aggression. And not just kids. What do we do with it? Do we harness it, or do we suppress it? Would that be a good topic?

EMMA Yes, it would. Can I give you a story to tell them? It will make a good starting point. It comes from a book I've been reading. The story comes out of Africa. "Every morning a gazelle wakes up. It knows that it must run faster than the fastest lion, or it will be killed. Every morning a lion wakes up. It knows that it must run faster than the slowest gazelle or it will starve to death. It doesn't matter whether you are a lion or a gazelle. When the sun comes up, you better start runnin'."

MARGARET I'm afraid Emma, that begs the question - just where do you run to? EMMA Margaret, talk sport. Kids follow that. Where do those William sisters run?

MARGARET To the winning post.

EMMA I agree boss. If you're afraid of failure you'll win nothing in life. You've got to zap those gremlins. You know what I think. There's just too many people out there that aspire to be mediocre. That's no way to be.

MARGARET Got no horizon? I'd put it another way. For our kids all their mountains are just a little bit higher, and someone has to keep reminding them about the view from the top.

Scene 6

TRACY Let's go back to our music lesson. Emma, Caribbean sunshine, was a wonderful teacher. She'd have been a great gospel singer in the Caribbean.

Music Room - a music lesson
Autumn 2002. Looking through the window it is now autumn.

Emma Kirk is sitting in front of Terry, Jean, Philippa and Tracy. Lesson illustrated by CD and DVD recordings

EMMA Our last lesson was all about mood and atmosphere created by music or captured in music. Can you remember any of it?

TERRY I remember *Mars God of War* from the *Planets*.

PHILIPPA Trust you to remember that one. I remember *Sinfonia Antarctica*.

It gave me the shivers.

EMMA Who was it by?

PHILIPPA Vaughan Williams.

EMMA Good, both of you. I'm really going to open up your ear drums this fine morning. The music I am going to play for you to today will reach parts of you that that well known beer won't reach.

TERRY Worth a try Miss. Give me one any day. PHILIPPA Oh shut up, Terry

EMMA I'm talking about the thing that separates the human race from the animal kingdom, music

TERRY Birds sing, don't they?

EMMA They're the exception that proves the rule. Wouldn't the world be awful if they didn't?

PHILIPPA Awful.

EMMA Anyway I'm talking today about the spiritual side of music. The spirit of God is in this music, or it's the human spirit. Call it either. In my book they are the same thing. It's the music of joy and the music of sadness. Discord as well as harmony. Carries the beat of life itself. We are going to start with harmony.

You see the great thing about music is that it has no boundaries. It is universal. Listen to **Music has no boundaries** sung by **Ladysmith Black Mambazo**.

(The music plays in the background during the rest of this scene.)

Those guys won two Grammies, and performed at two Nobel Peace Prize ceremonies.

That piece of music comes out of South Africa, but If you want to find your God, if there is a God, listen to good music from anywhere in the big wide world.

(Music ends)

Scene 7

Office of the Director of Education
There is a desk and chair in one corner, and also a round table with 4 chairs. David Harding is joined first by SEN Officer, Gerry Thompson.

MARGARET Not too late I hope?

DAVID Not at all. Take a seat. Can I come straight to the point of our meeting? MARGARET Sure.

DAVID It's a bit – how should I put it? - delicate. Can I rely on your discretion? MARGARET I suppose - how delicate?

DAVID Well, really very delicate.

MARGARET Oh dear. You had better break it to me then.

DAVID You know we need to close your school.

MARGARET I was hoping that the parents might have persuaded you to change your mind.

DAVID Their campaign wasn't a waste of time. It forced us to address the closure much more seriously. We do realise that we have got to work very hard to make sure that your kids don't lose out.

GERRY We can't afford to have a hundred angry parents on our back.

DAVID You think that more than half of your roll could do really well in mainstream schools?

MARGARET Yes, if you prepared properly for them... trained the staff to take them... .put an end to bullying ... and give them the attention and the time they need.

DAVID We are going to do all of that, aren't we Gerry?

GERRY Yes, that's in hand. We're getting some great success stories.

MARGARET Yes, you parade them like Lotto winners.

GERRY That's unfair.

MARGARET But it's true. Are you stopping bullying? Have you read how much there is of it today? Nearly every kid with special needs is bullied in mainstream schools at one time or another? It's always the most vulnerable on the receiving end of it.

GERRY It is in hand.

MARGARET Do you realise that every time you fail, bullying may blight the entire life of one of our youngsters. Do you realise that?

GERRY It's in hand, Margaret.

MARGARET Gerry, get real, For our kids it's not just a learning experience that they all have to go through, you know. It can be a life sentence. And when you know the number of attempted suicides in youngsters every year, it can be a short life too. GERRY We are tackling it, Margaret. We know we have to.

DAVID We certainly do, for the kids' sake, and to persuade parents to go along with us. We have to have parents on our side, not on our backs. Believe me.

GERRY That's what we are talking about today. We have a sort of plan.

DAVID I'll come straight to the point. We want you to sell the closure of the School to parents and staff.

MARGARET Last time you asked me to back you up. Now you're asking me

to do the whole job for you. The answer is no, definitely no. Why won't you take no for an answer?

DAVID Things have moved on since last time.

MARGARET What things?

GERRY We're better prepared. We've listened to your parents.

MARGARET Come on Gerry, you've written a few more concept papers.
GERRY That's not fair. Training for special needs has started in mainstream schools. And with teaching assistants we are giving one to one help to a lot of kids.

MARGARET One to point one, more like. Who's training who, Gerry?

GERRY Physio's are training teaching assistants and some mums too.

MARGARET Wonderful, and they'll have no time for their clients. It won't be hands on for them, it will be hands off. You can't mass produce professional skills, you know. Or do you think you can? Do you think you're a miracle man? Stop fooling yourself, Gerry.

GERRY Please don't be so negative. Head teachers say they are prepared.

MARGARET Negative, negative, they say what you want them to say. Look, I gave a lot of thought to this last year. I don't want to take sides in this. It's not my job. It's yours, not mine. It's yours. I'm just not prepared to do it for you. I can't betray my own school like that, not after the parents' campaign to keep it open. I can't and you shouldn't be asking me to.

DAVID Margaret, we are asking you to face the reality of the situation, and get parents to do the same.

GERRY How many did your roll drop by last year? MARGARET Nine.

GERRY I hear its going to drop by another fourteen this year. MARGARET It certainly will if you keep kids from being admitted.

GERRY We don't stop them. We help them go to mainstream schools. And it will get worse for you. With fewer pupils and our new banding scheme you are going to have to face some big budget cuts. There'll have to be redundancies. Or you'll simply lose staff as they look around for greater job security and advancement. And you won't be able to replace them. I don't know whether you've heard but your Music Teacher, Emma Kirk's her name, yes?

MARGARET Yes

DAVID She'll shortly be leaving you, a regional appointment. It's a big step up for her.

MARGARET Something tells me you're way ahead of me here.

DAVID If we are, you'll soon catch up.

MARGARET The school is to wither on the vine?

GERRY Your words not ours. But it's got to happen anyway. You must see that.

MARGARET I do, all too clearly.

DAVID Will you help us? if you do, you'll end up with a much better chance of a headship elsewhere. There's one coming up in the next couple of years in Grovewood Comprehensive School. And there may be a job for your English teacher too. We do have a little influence in these things, you know.

MARGARET I really don't know whether I'm hearing you right. Are you seriously saying that you want me to betray my kids?

DAVID Not betray them. Look to their best long term interests.

GERRY We don't want another public confrontation between the school and the LEA. That's no good for anyone, is it? And it can't be good for you or your colleagues. It just sours everything when we are trying to pull together and get things right for your kids.

DAVID Sometimes you have to be cruel to be kind.

MARGARET You admit that you're being cruel.

DAVID But I am trying to be kind. That's the way that things get done.

MARGARET And people get done, David.

GERRY Margaret, just look two years ahead. Fewer kids. Less money. Fewer staff. Do you think you personally, never mind the school, can face an OFSTED inspection.

MARGARET Give me the weekend to think it over. Please.

DAVID No. (*emphatically*) No, I'm not going to do that. For your sake. You'll only prolong the agony of making the decision you know you have to make. I'm sure we've said nothing you haven't already thought about, thought about a lot.

MARGARET (*under her breath*) Damn your eyes.

GERRY Don't you see it. We don't just want your voice. We want your expertise too. You know the way its going. I've got a little working party to progress it. Join us. There couldn't be a better way to help your kids than that.

MARGARET Come on Gerry, if you really wanted me you'd have asked me before now. You only really like people on your committees who agree with you.

DAVID Please, Margaret.

MARGARET I register a protest on behalf of the Governors and the parents.
DAVID That will be for them, Margaret. But you'll go along with us?

MARGARET I will not give you the satisfaction of thinking you've persuaded me. I will not... (*pause*) But, I'll go along with you. Okay.

Scene 8

TRACY I suppose that's the real world. When you're at school it isn't there.

In the music room

TERRY Do you really believe in God, Miss?

EMMA Well if she does exist, she wears many different costumes.

PHILIPPA I thought God was a "him".

TRACY "Hymns is what you sing to God."

PHILIPPA A "He" then.

EMMA God is whatever you want God to be: He, She or It.

TERRY My dad doesn't believe that God exists.

HARRY My dad does. Speak for yourself Terry.

EMMA She doesn't if you don't believe in her. She does if you do. My folk believed in God and saw God as the Father. For me though, God is a mother. After all, mothers know all about the pain of creation, don't they? The Bible's a great book. But there's far too many men in it. Anyway I'm not sure that 'believe' is the right word. I know she's there. The spirit of God is in every living thing. You just have to listen out for her. But you can turn your back on her too. It's your choice.

TERRY I've chosen. (*He gives the thumbs down sign*)

EMMA When you listen to more music you may change your mind. I believe that the hand of God has actually touched the great composers and musicians, and made them great, and for certain not the hand of Charlie Darwin. I heard that great opera singer Placido Domingo say he believed his voice came from God. Music comes up from the earth itself - just listen to this – monks singing in Tibet (**Giving and taking by Tibetan monks of Garden Shartse & Corciolli.**) And it can come up from the sands of the desert. (**Sufi music.**)

(The music continues softly for a while as the lesson continues)

Those voices come right out of God's good earth, don't they? They remind us that we don't just take from the earth, we have to give back to it.

Ha I've heard that music at home. I've chosen Miss.

EMMA Sure you have. That music comes from deep down in the earth, but it reaches right up to those angels in Heaven –Can you tell me a piece of heavenly music?

TERRY 'Ave… a Bloody Mary

EMMA Now I'll have no blaspheming in my class. Say "Ave Maria" Terry.

TERRY Ave Maria Terry.

EMMA That's a little better. Another one?

PHILIPPA I heard "Agnus Dei" on Classic FM. I think by Faure. It was so lovely.

EMMA Very good. That's part of the Faure Requiem. You see, you guys, there's the joy of the human spirit and there's tragedy. You know the Holocaust, where millions of Jews, gypsies, and kids just like you were murdered because they didn't belong to the master race. Listen to (**John William's) Schindler's List.**

(The music continues softly until "I'm beginning to…)

TRACY That's really sad.

PHILIPPA I don't think it's spiritual though.

TERRY And where was God Miss when all that murdering was going on? If he was a good God he would have put a stop to it.

EMMA The Bible gives answer, Terry. Folk remember Adam and Eve in the Garden of Eden. They forget the serpent. God couldn't stop Adam and Eve listenin' to that serpent and then eatin' the forbidden apple. You see God had given them the choice of eatin' or not eatin'.

TERRY Why didn't he put a worm in it then?

EMMA Oh Terry. It wasn't God who had the choice. It was man. But God was there. Yes, right there in those terrible concentration camps, keeping the hope alive of the tiny few who survived. That sure wasn't easy, keeping hope alive in that hell-hole amongst the huge piles of bones and carcasses and the stench of it all.

TERRY Bloody funny God.

EMMA Terry, listen, God was with the Quakers when they rescued thousands of Jewish children from Hitler's Germany before the war, and saved them from the gas chambers. I read about one Jewish boy. His family was gassed. He survived and he became a cantor in a synagogue in Glasgow. He kept his faith alive in Auschwitz, making a candle with the oil of an empty sardine tin. That's the power of faith. God was there Terry, He was with that man as I am here. And that's why God feels our sadness now. When I listen to that music I feel that sadness. Don't you feel it, Philippa?

PHILIPPA I'm beginning to.

EMMA Close your eyes. Terry, close your eyes. You too, Come on you heathen. Imagine you're on my island in the Caribbean. Think of the ebb and flow of the tides lappin' the shore, the rippling streams that flow into the turbulent oceans. Harry imagine the world your dad comes from, the rocks and boulders that shape its mountains, all of nature – its unbelievable beauty, its incredible power, just its infinite variety –nature's awesome wonders.

PHILIPPA I love David Attenborough's programmes on the telly.

EMMA Yes, Philippa, these are for ever God's gifts to you and to me, to all mankind. Without distinction between believer and unbeliever, between rich and poor. And you guys, they are for ever, for ever. (*Very softly then absolute silence*)

TERRY (*Drops drum stick*) Sorry. Miss.

EMMA Never mind. God's just left the room!

TRACY I am not sure that God ever came back. (*Pause*) Come back in fifteen minutes. I'll tell you the rest of the story.

ACT TWO

Scene 1

Head teacher's living room
There is a small couch and two easy chairs, CD player and a bookcase. A bottle of wine is on the table with a glass. Margaret Wiliiamson is on her own to begin with. She is joined by John Errington who lets himself in.

MARGARET Help yourself to a glass of wine. JOHN Yes, I will

MARGARET It's been a hell of a bad week, one of my worst downers for a long time. Tommy Dixon.

JOHN Only thirteen, a great kid.

MARGARET Then Jean Rutherford's mum wanted more speech and language therapy for her child, but just not available.

JOHN You can't produce it out of the hat, can you?

MARGARET Exactly. I wish I could. I lost my cool, and she lost hers. She said she'd report me to the Governors. I can really do without that. Then another parent, Terry James's father, said he wanted to report Emma to the Governors, and we can all do without that too.

JOHN Emma? I thought everyone loved our music teacher?

MARGARET Not this time. She's been propagating her Pentecostal ideas in her music lessons. That's what Mr. James alleges. He says he's an atheist and he objects. Then for good measure he said that if he was a Christian he'd also object. Emma believes God is a woman and he said that's heresy.

JOHN Poor Emma. She can't win either way. Did you discuss it with her?
MARGARET Yes, of course I did. She insisted that she was not propagating her faith, she was just describing it, and was entitled to her opinions. She said the Singhs were very interested in her religion and dad's a Sikh. I think they both follow the Sikh faith. Well I had to tell her she lived in an age of political correctness, and she had to keep her opinions to herself.

JOHN I'll bet Emma didn't go along with that.

MARGARET She did not, and it got quite heated. We're supposed to be educating these kids, she shouted. They have to learn how to agree and how to disagree. How can I teach them if you gag me? And she went out slamming the door. Then the 'phone rang. I had a really distraught mum complaining about the LEA. She's wanted her son admitted to this school for ages. The LEA will admit him to almost any other one.

JOHN Another one?

MARGARET Yes. You wouldn't believe what her son's been doing - smearing his crap all over the walls of the house.

JOHN Poor woman.

MARGARET Sheer frustration if you ask me. I am sure we could do something for that boy. And mum is having to deal with this all on her own.

JOHN Well that's the sort of thing that happens when the LEA decides to starve a school of pupils.

MARGARET It is. The real problem is the LEA. And they actually want me to work with them to close the school… to try and prove to the parents that the school just isn't viable.

JOHN Oh, not again. Don't they understand basic economics. The more kids in this school the less each one costs?

MARGARET They do not. I wouldn't trust them with my household budget. I'd be in the knackers' yard in a week. It's just that in their simple little minds they think that all our kids would be better off in mainstream schools.

JOHN Oh dear. That's terrible. Some yes, maybe, not all, not all.

MARGARET I don't like letting the school down, but you can't fight them, can you? They are bound to win in the end whatever our parents say.

JOHN What do they want you to do?

MARGARET Just argue their case for them, the case for Inclusion. They think it will be more persuasive if I say it than if they do.

JOHN They're certainly not wrong about that.

MARGARET And they're going to make it easier for me. Easier! We are going to run short of money with falling rolls and budget cuts. There'll have to be redundancies. Everything I've worked for. My God. And I've got to applaud it. You know they even suggested I took down our Merit Board. They said you can't live in the past. Give me a hug.

(They snuggle up together on the couch)

MARGARET I think I know the answer.

JOHN What?

MARGARET I'll resign.

JOHN That's a silly thing to do.

MARGARET No, it's not. It's the only thing to do.

JOHN Just put that idea right out of your head.

MARGARET Don't you understand. I'm pig sick of this job. And I'm pig sick of the world we're living in. Every damn thing is a cynical charade, and I'm now given a lead role.

JOHN If everyone who didn't like their job resigned, there'd be a hell of a lot of vacancies.

MARGARET Don't you understand, I just can't do it any longer. I can't look my kids in the face. I can't look my staff in the face, or the governors. And, what's more, I can't look myself in the face either.

JOHN You must.

MARGARET I can't.

JOHN What about us?

MARGARET What about us? It won't make any difference if I'm not here.
JOHN Of course it will make a difference. But anyway it's a waste. You're a wonderful teacher and a wonderful head. You can't give all that up.

What about your pension? What are you going to live on? What will you do with yourself?

MARGARET I'll find something. I won't be the first teacher to throw in the towel. Now will I?

JOHN Look, whoever takes your place will do what you've said you'd do, and probably without any conscience at all. What on earth are you going to gain?

MARGARET My conscience. My sanity!

JOHN Oh, come on. That's self indulgence.

MARGARET Self Indulgence. Self indulgence. Oh my god. How can you say that to me? You of all people. What a horrid thing to say. I don't think you understand me at all. I want out. I want out altogether. Out, out, out.

JOHN You're just trying to make a martyr of yourself.

MARGARET If that's the best thing you can say you'd better go.

JOHN Oh, be sensible.

MARGARET Go... Please go. Just get out of my life.

JOHN I just hope and pray you'll come to your senses. In a year's time all this will be a bad dream.

MARGARET Just leave me alone. Leave me alone. Get out of my life.

(John exits with her head down)

Scene 2

TRACY The next evening Mummy Margaret tried to kill herself. I'll never forget the next day... not ever. The School was in mourning. I've never seen everyone look so sad. It was awful. Awful. It must have been terrible for her. We still didn't know for sure whether our head teacher was OK or not. There was a rumour that it had something to do with closing our school. Emma gave us all a hug. She said she was praying every minute of the day for our head teacher. Terry went home. He was sick all over the place. Wendy had to clear up the mess. And me? I was all weepy, and I didn't feel like learning anything at all that day That day someone trod on my dreams.

In the Director's office
David Harding picks up the telephone.

DAVID .... Morning, Don. How are you?... Any spare time on your hands? We need your help?.... Good... I am pleased to say she is. They've brought her round.... It's a bit complicated. I'll try to explain. You know we've been trying to close Brighouse for some time... Yes, more than a little, and the governors too... You know us too well. ... Take over the school for six months, maybe a year...... We want you to sell the closure to the governors and the parents. You may find the Governors a bit difficult... Yes, they must know their place... weren't you a canny spin bowler too if I remember it, take seven wickets for thirty once? ... No-one said it wasn't cricket (*Gentle laughter*) ... many thanks. Gerry Thompson will be in touch with you to take it forward. Bye. And, just watch that bicycle of yours. We certainly can't afford another of our head teachers risking life and limb. Okay mate.

(David puts down the phone and immediately picks it up again.)

DAVID James. Glad I've caught you. I thought you should know. The head of Brighouse has tried to kill herself ... No, mercifully not ... silly old what?... I am not sure who is the silly old thing ... No, I haven't lost control .... Yes, I am upset ... and so should you be. It could have been a disaster. ... I agree it isn't... It's actually opportunistic. We are putting one of our own people into the school to head it up, Don Smithson. .... Yes, I am sure the governors will go along with it. .... No I won't lose any sleep. ... Just thought you should know. Bye. *(Puts phone down)* And so he damn well should.

Scene 3

TRACY Well, Mr. Smithson took over as head, we were told until Mummy Margaret was well enough to come back. I called him Daddy-long-legs in my diary. It was amazing how quickly our lessons got back to normal.

Music Room - a music lesson continued – Spring 2003
TERRY But God's gifts kill.

EMMA They also heal. You can't have a world just made out of sugar candy.
TERRY It's more like my mam's suet pudding.

PHILIPPA Do you pray to God?

EMMA Do I pray to her? Well I know that lots of folk don't, and they can tell me I am a nutter, but I talk to Her every day.

TERRY My Dad thinks that people who hear voices are bonkers. EMMA He thinks what he thinks. I think what I know.

TRACY My Nana used to say that God was as near to her as a new born babe and as far away as the furthest star?

EMMA I like your Nana. She was a wise one, that lady. She knew, like I do.
PHILIPPA Do you pray for this school?

EMMA Sure I do. Every single day I pray for this school, and I pray for you.
TERRY My mam said you're leaving us.

TRACY No!

EMMA Gossip. I'll have no gossiping in my class. Some people have nothing better to do than wag their tongues. Today I'm going to play you some spiritual music from my part of the world by my childhood hero, Paul Robeson. People used to call it a slave song. **Deep River** Now I'm goin' to tell you a little story about Paul Robeson. I remember my Daddyo recounting how he heard the great Black American singer in Peekskill, a little town in New York State, at a big open air concert. You know, not everyone likes being told that they are all God's children. There's always some that don't. And on that day those folk came out in force with their clubs, their rocks and their stones, and they rained them down on those peaceful concert goers. On little children too, as they made their way home.

TRACY No. Why did they do a terrible thing like that?

EMMA Well, some people just don't believe in a universal creator. They believe in their own tribal God. That's always making for trouble and suffering. Anyway, that's all half a century ago. I'm sure times have changed in Westchester County. But what Paul Robeson said about folk music fifty years ago is just as true today. Let's get back to it. You see, one of the earliest gifts God gave to mankind was music.

TERRY Was it a Christmas present Miss?

EMMA Oh for heaven's sake, Terry, it was a gift to Christian, Jew, Muslim, Buddhist, Hindu, Sikh and to non-believer from that day to this - no-one any different. It was a gift then and it's a gift today, to every new born child.

Now let's round this lesson off with one more piece of fine spiritual music to help you understand all this a bit better. The voices you'll hear carry the spirit of God in them or, if you want, simply the human spirit. Take your pick. Either way enjoy, enjoy. Just listen to this: **Hallelujah Chorus from Handel's Messiah.**

(Hallelujah Chorus until the end of the scene)

TRACY Wow

PHILIPPA I really don't know whether I believe or I don't… but I know that I'd really like to.

EMMA You guys will never be alone in life when you have found music. And one other thing. If you listen to spiritual music, really listen, you won't worship a tribal God, you'll worship God, the creator of everythin' and everyone. A God that will heal the wounds of mankind.

TERRY That would be a fuckin' miracle.

EMMA Terry**,** don't use that word in my classroom. Don't use it ever again…. But, for once, I am agreein' with you. People shouldn't just pray together when they mourn their dead in war.

Scene 4

TRACY I'm afraid the good times didn't last. There turned out to be truth in the rumour that our music teacher was going to leave us. And worse. There mightn't be a full time music teacher taking her place. And there was another rumour. The LEA still wanted to close us down. I've still got the letter I wrote to the Prime Minister. I thought I could make it a special wheelchair delivery to Downing Street, but I just posted it. Jean said she'd make a news story out of it in the Gazette. It got a little write up there.

"Dear Prime Minister

I am writing to invite you to visit my school. I am writing to you personally because you should know what pupils like me think about where we should be taught. I know that some love the big challenge of a mainstream school. We think we will be much better off here, learning more and enjoying our school days as well. You should see for yourself just how much we will lose if this school is closed. My parents told me this could still happen, even though all our parents said that they wanted it kept open. My childhood was a happy one, but difficult at the same time. When you are in a wheel chair and all your friends have been walking, straight away it clicks you're different. I first went to a primary school, but I was called "old wheelie bin" there, and that was not very pleasant. Some friends of mine were called "spackers."

Then I came here to Brighouse. They gave me real enthusiasm for living. Brighouse does not take or give the easy option. It pushes everyone to the full and then pushes some more. They pushed me academically and physically, even though I am in a wheel chair. My pals have competed in Great North Runs, and in the Athens Paralympics. One won a Silver medal there, and another a Gold. And I am planning to get my GCSE's and word processing qualifications. I also play in the Tin Pan Ally Steel Drum Band. We have gigs every week and give a lot of pleasure to a lot of people and especially to ourselves. Children like me don't want to be social experiments. We have got one chance and the staff here know how to make it a real one. If you could just spare the time to come down to our school, and look into the eyes of the children and ask them where they want to be, I personally guarantee you won't want us to go anywhere else. I may not be a voter today. But I soon will be.

Yours sincerely,
Tracy Jones

Scene 5

TRACY I got a long letter back, not from the Prime Minister. We wouldn't lose out. Our parents would be fully consulted. De da, de da, de da.. You know, in Downing Street, that's the one thing the faceless ones are very good at....writing letters. The terrible cloud over the school began to lift a little. Mummy Margaret had come round. It didn't lift altogether though, not for anyone. For a start Mummy Margaret had to learn to live with herself.

One month later
In Margaret Williamson's living room, Margaret is listening to Lizst's

"Consolations". She has asked Eileen Winterton, chair of Governors, to call in to see her. The door bell rings and Margaret answers it.

MARGARET Do come on in. I am so pleased you could come.

(Margaret switches off music as Eileen walks into the room.)

MARGARET Do tell me. How are things at the school?

EILEEN We're managing fine. Your stand in, Don Smithson.

MARGARET He's a good egg.

EILEEN Yes, the LEA really helped us, suggesting we called him in. He's getting the show back on the road. The kids like him a lot.

MARGARET I am sure the staff do too. He's not a stranger to them.

EILEEN Meanwhile how are you?

MARGARET A bit better than I have been, and a little worse than I could be.

EILEEN I was hoping you would say you're much better.

MARGARET Well I certainly could be.

EILEEN You gave us all a terrible shock.

We lost Frank Jones you know.

MARGARET I'd heard that.

EILEEN He was as upset as anyone. Keeping an eye on finance for us. He's a big loss. Your er, it was the straw that broke the camel's back. He resigned at our last Governors' meeting. Said it was pressure of business.

MARGARET Oh.

EILEEN I think he felt that the LEA was at the bottom of it all. He's a quiet chap. But he exploded at the meeting. You know Gerry Thompson was there introducing Don Smithson. He said the LEA was stopping kids coming to Brighouse even though parents wanted them there.

MARGARET True.

EILEEN Well, salami tactics, he called it. Then, looking straight at Gerry he said he was a Rotarian committed to high ethical standards in business and the professions and the Local Education Authority needed a lesson or two. Then he left us.

MARGARET Did Gerry say anything?

EILEEN Nothing he could say. I just had the feeling that he felt he had one less person to worry about.

MARGARET Well, I am very sorry my little troubles led to all that. Anyway, I thought I owed you an explanation. That's why I invited you round.

EILEEN Yes, I feel I should know, if you do want to talk about it. But I did quiz John a couple of weeks ago.

MARGARET Oh. It's still better to get it first hand if you can. Always a bit more reliable that way.

EILEEN Do you really want it that way? I didn't want to bother you with a whole lot of questions.

MARGARET I need it that way.

Door bell rings and Margaret opens it.

JOHN I'm sorry if I'm interrupting you. I wanted to borrow one of your books. Actually to lend to Tracy. Nesbit's "Beautiful Stories from Shakespeare."

MARGARET If you're going to lend someone a book, it's a very good idea to lend someone else's. Do help yourself. (*John goes across to bookshelf and removes book.*)

EILEEN I don't mind if John stays, if he'd like to.

MARGARET Would you like to? I was just explaining to Eileen why I did what I did.

JOHN No, no, I'll leave you to it.

MARGARET Do stay.

JOHN Okay. If you'd like me to.

MARGARET I've had to ask myself quite a few questions. You know the most awful moment? It wasn't taking the overdose. You sort of reconcile yourself to that. The most awful moment is when you wake up and a nurse is offering you a cup of tea. The nightmare returns, you see. You have to face up to everything all over again, and added to that, there's what you have tried to do and failed. That's when you really hit the bottom... and weep.

JOHN Did you find some help?

MARGARET Yes I did. There was a most wonderful young Indian doctor. A psychiatrist. I was so grateful to him. He listened, which was the most important thing to me at the time. He just listened while I talked, and I needed to. It helped.

EILEEN I am so glad.

MARGARET Then he started talking. He introduced me to Ayerveda.

JOHN I've never heard of it.

MARGARET It's a 5000-year-old science from India. They believe that everyone has three doshas, sort of undercurrents to your being. The essence is to find a balance. The way to cope with life, and the nasties it sometimes throws at you, is to find your true self, accept it, be comfortable with it, yes with all of its imperfections, despite them. And the really difficult bit, you have to forgive them, one by one. I could only find peace within myself if I could do this.

JOHN I thought you suddenly realised you'd be lost without the kids, totally lost, you know unable to help them, that whatever you did you were losing all that.

EILEEN And a bit depressed too about what's going on in schools today. Life just not worth living.

MARGARET Maybe there's a grain of truth in that. People prattle on about equality of opportunity, but what our kids need is just opportunity, and a helping hand from us to find it.

JOHN Some compassion too.

MARGARET Yes, sure. Kids are all equally important, but they are all different. They need different opportunities. Anyway, it wasn't just all of that that got to me. There is a stronger more destructive emotion than despair, you know. Hate. Hate...

JOHN Oh! *(in surprise)*

MARGARET Yes, don't you see? I hated the world and what it was doing to these kids. I hated its *(searching for a word)* mediocrity. I hated myself for betraying them. I hated my imperfections. For a moment, I even hated you John. It's that hatred I have to cleanse out of my system. Better than taking Prozac and all those other pills.

EILEEN I am beginning to see the importance of this afternoon to you.

MARGARET Part of this had to be sharing the truth with you, making my peace with you and with the school. I have to tell you, you see. They leant on me to tell parents the school had to close. They asked me to drop a bomb on my own school, on everything I've tried to build. And I agreed to do it. I hated me. Do you see?

JOHN It wasn't just as you said to me, that you felt like a little lump of plasticine in the hands of the LEA?

EILEEN It went well beyond that?

MARGARET Yes. You know what that Indian doctor helped me to see. The real antidote to despair, to hatred to anger. You know what it is? The gift of love. That's actually what we give our kids.

JOHN Emma would call it the gift from God.

MARGARET I just call it the gift from us. John, one thing I must ask you. Have you forgiven me?

JOHN Well, almost. Your note. (*Remembering the pain.*) Oh.

MARGARET Only almost? Oh dear.

EILEEN What was that lovely piece of music you were playing as I arrived?

MARGARET It's called "Consolations." Emma sent it to me with her best wishes, and from the kids in her class too. I really appreciated that.

EILEEN Play it again.

(*Margaret puts on the CD It runs into the next scene. She puts her house key on the table and after a long moment, John picks it up and puts it in his pocket.*

Scene 6

Left Stage

TRACY I've tried to understand it. Why do some people like to destroy things that are beautiful? They do. They really do. Some are just out and out vandals. What they can't have, they don't want anyone else to have. But others? Maybe it's because they think that what's right for them is right for everyone else, when it just isn't, and then they go on to think that everything else is wrong. If that is the reason, they make a big mistake. When you think about it, isn't it a bit arrogant? A bit blinkered? Aren't they - how do you say – sometimes just too clever by half? Certainly too clever for our good. It isn't as though they've always got it right for the kids that want to go to mainstream schools and there are some. Somebody should tell them. The trouble is that they think they understand us. They just don't, and they don't understand what they are stealing from some of us either. The rest of this play is history. It started with a meeting with the parents and the execution squad. I wasn't invited.

David Harding's Office. David makes two phone calls.

DAVID Don – Thank's mate for last night … it wasn't nothing… It'll be a great relief for the ruling party. You and Gerry really did calm the stormy waters …. Yes, … we're putting the wheels in motion straightaway… Good man … You deserve it. I won't keep you. Cheers, mate.

DAVID Judy, You Okay? … I've got some good news for you about Brighouse School. The dogs of war are back in their kennels. Yes … We had a meeting with parents last night …Yes, one or two did bark, but their bark was worse than their bite. … Well, obviously some parents weren't very happy … bullying in mainstream, I'd say. It's not as though we don't know about that. Gerry's got it in hand … Don Smithson did us proud. … No, Governors are on board too … We had a meeting with them last week. Don explained that half a school wasn't better than none. … Yes, I suppose Margaret's absence was a blessing in disguise… she's much better these days… Anyway, do pass this on to our friends in London. Tell them they can take us off their hit list.

Scene 7

TRACY Well, it had to happen, didn't it? It was about a year later. Have you ever seen a bulldozer at work? You must have. And have you heard it clanking and grinding? I still can. One moment a building is there. Almost the next it is a pile of rubble, just rubble. And we watched it all happen. I won't forget it. I lost part of myself that day. That bulldozer, well for me, it was sort of symbolic. You see we were all casualties one way or another. Remember the name my friends call me, Katy, after Kate Winslet. I was on the Titanic, too.

A year later

The scene is outside the School. A bulldozer is slowly demolishing the building. Staff, parents and children watch. John Errington and Margaret Williamson have come in together. They are followed by Emma Kirk and Eileen Winterton. All are wearing raincoats.

JOHN Oh God, politicians. Save us from politicians. Scurvy politicians, that's how William Shakespeare described them.

EMMA Jesus Christ said "Forgive them, for they know not what they do".
JOHN Sorry Emma, I really can't bring myself to do that.

EILEEN I am a bit surprised to see you here. EMMA I owed it to my memories. It's so sad. JOHN Yes, so very sad

MARGARET I just felt I had to come. I still wonder whether I could have done anything to prevent this.

EMMA Oh for heaven's sake, now don't you say that. This was always going to happen. We all did our best for the kids one way or another. Anyway, how are you keeping?

MARGARET It's not easy. Good days and bad, but more good than bad, and the medics said I could get back to work. I feel much more like it now. And it's good for me.

EILEEN We all hope so too. You are a wonderful Head. The kids love you. And you really stretched them, and you made them whole, whole human beings.

MARGARET They made me whole. And they stretched me too. I'm applying for a job in the new Academy. I hope that the medics say I am fit enough for that. The LEA thinks I have a good chance to get it, especially with my experience of special needs, and they are short of head teachers these days.

EILEEN You carry all our good wishes. You know that.

MARGARET I do and I am grateful for them.

EILEEN Hopefully some of our kids will get into the Academy.

MARGARET They better had.

EILEEN You hope to go there too John?

JOHN If they'll have me. It's either that or Grovewood Comp.

MARGARET That's my alternative too. It does need to be one of them.

(Jean, Philippa, Terry and Tracy arrive together, the bulldozer noise intensifies.)

TRACY It's a crime

PHILIPPA It's a waste.

JEAN I think it's obscene.

TERRY They're all shit.

MARGARET Terry, you shouldn't use that word in polite company.

TERRY Very sorry miss. Those pills can't be working.

MARGARET The money was wasted on you, Terry.

(Enter RANJIT and Harry, bulldozer noise temporarily stops.)

EMMA No Judith with you?

RANJIT Hospital duty calls.

HARRY I don't understand.

RANJIT I don't either. Kids have just one chance, and they spoil it for them with their big ideas. And another thing. They try to make us feel guilty doin' the best for our kids, givin' good schools like this a bad name as a reason for pulling them down.

EMMA They don't understand. That's the trouble. They don't begin to understand. Schools like this have the gift of healing. They engage the spirit. They are for life. That's what's so good about them.

MARGARET Emma, some people don't want to understand.

RANJIT I wish someone would expose the charade of those who say they care. They just don't.

MARGARET No, that's not quite right. Some do care. They do, you know. It's just that they care more about defending their precious little cardboard castles, and then helping others defend theirs.

RANJIT You've hit the nail on the head there. Rights of kids paramount. Words. Empty words. They invite us to their meetings, but they don't listen to what we are saying.

(Bulldozer noises continue in the background until the end of the scene)

HARRY What about all those prayers to God, Miss? They don't seem to work.

EMMA We are not given to understand everything, Harry. At times her ways are very inscrutable.

HARRY What does "inscrutable" mean?

EMMA Well, in my book God's a woman. Sometimes you just don't know whether She's coming or going. Women are like that. They're wired differently. Same power source as men, but different. You'll find out when you're a little older.

HARRY So are you still going to sing her praises on Sunday?

EMMA Sure I am. She knows how I feel. It's just She's got some catching up to do. JOHN Emma dear, please, you really don't have to bring God into it.

EMMA I do bring God into it. I just fear for her temper these days. One way or another - I think we're really provokin' her. She's capable of quite a tantrum when she's provoked. We'd better be a bit more careful with ourselves, and stop provokin' her.

TERRY You're right. Just like my Dad.

JOHN Well I won't disagree with you…, God or no God.

TRACY In a year's time there'll be some lovely houses here.

HARRY I bag the house with our duck pond.

MARGARET Rubble, just rubble. Such a pity.

JOHN Memories, just memories.

EMMA Come on you guys, join me, like good old times. (*Everyone singing*) "You are my sunshine, my only sunshine; you **made** me happy, when skies **were** grey.

ALL You'll never know dear, how much I loved you...please don't take my sunshine away."

Bulldozer continues its demolition. Time for quiet contemplation.

TRACY Remember the little white dandelion heads blowing away in the wind. Well, a couple of weeks ago, in the next street to mine, a boy of twelve – I think he was a bit overweight – well, he tried to take his own life. Thank you for coming to listen to my story. Can I leave you with a really naughty thought to take home with you. There are some little creatures that build and defend their own nests but they cannot move on and they cannot do anything else. That's what they do. They build and defend their own nests. That's all they do That's all they've ever done. That's all they'll ever do. There is a name for them. "*Termites*", yes "*Termites*." If there are any of them here tonight, let them go to their beds and sleep peacefully … if they can. Y'see I'm not just going to blow away in the wind. Good night.

From Alice in Blunderland

The Mad Hatter's Committee Meeting

The Mad Hatter was in the Chair. "Order, Order" he cried, and Disorder clumped noisily out of the room.

"The Minutes of the last meeting" he said imperiously.

The White Knight asked which Minutes he wanted. "The Minutes that go on for days and days, the Minutes that go on for hours, or the Minutes that go on only for seconds?"

"That's a difficult one" said the Mad Hatter. "Shall we take the Minutes as read?"

"I can't read." said Doormouse.

"Pretend to." said the Mad Hatter.

"How do you pretend to?" said Doormouse still reluctant to agree.

"Like you always do." said the Mad Hatter, getting just a little bit irritated.

Alice looked around the table. It was a well attended meeting. The March Hare, the Cheshire Cat, the White Rabbit, the White Queen, The Knave of Hearts, Caterpillar, Tweedledum and Tweedledee were all in their place. Doormouse was under his.

And a very small black fly had settled on the wall behind the Mad Hatter's Chair.

"The Minutes are agreed." said the Mad Hatter.

"Apologies for absence?" asked the Mad Hatter. "Humpty Dumpty" said the White Knight. "He had a serious accident since we last met."

"Any Correspondence? " asked the Mad Hatter.

"Yes, two matters" replied the White Knight. "we have just had a new Plan from the Ogre Queen. It's on the table. It is an all singing and dancing Plan."

Alice noticed that an attractive book on the table suddenly started dancing a highland jig and at the same time sang the Hallelujah Chorus from Handel's Messiah.

"What's in the Plan?" asked the Cheshire Cat.

"There's meetings". "Great." said the Cheshire Cat. "New partnerships.". "Wonderful." said Caterpillar. "And there's much more delusion." said the Mad Hatter. "Don't you mean Inclusion?" said the White Knight. "A Freudian slip. said the Mad Hatter with a wry smile.

"I move we buy it."

"Can we afford it?" asked Doormouse suddenly waking up.

"We get paid to buy it, twice the actual cost" said the White Knight helpfully.

"I am still not sure we can afford it" said Doormouse.

"Go back to sleep" said the Mad Hatter. And Doormouse did as he was told.

"Then that's agreed?" Nods all round, including Doormouse who was nodding away with the rest of them.

"What's the other letter?" asked the Mad Hatter.

"We are going to be inspected by the two blind mice." Said White Knight.

"My God" said the March Hare. "No, by two blind mice" said the White Knight..

"I thought there were three of them" said Caterpillar, suddenly getting a word in edgeways.

"One of them has just had a successful cataract operation" said the White Knight. "Why isn't he here then?" asked Caterpillar. "He's back in hospital with post traumatic shock … seeing things for the first time knocked him gaga."

Alice noticed that that the visit from the two blind mice caused no great concern. "Aren't you worried?" She asked.

"We've just bought the Plan" said the Mad Hatter.

"Off with our heads if we hadn't" observed the March Hare.

Alice saw that everyone was laughing hilariously.

"Let's get down to the main business of the meeting" said the Mad Hatter. "There is a resolution on the table, moved by the Knave of Hearts and seconded by the March Hare. - 'The Moon is made of cheese' - Knave of Hearts over to you."

"I like cheese and I can't do without it" started the Knave of Hearts. "Not totally relevant" said Caterpillar. "Not relevant maybe, but important" replied the Knave of Hearts, just a trifle aggressively.

"Anyway" he continued, "you can see for yourself it's made of cheese. It's round."

At this point the March Hare intervened. "I second the motion." he said firmly. "I have the evidence. I've been given a piece." "Where is it then?" asked Alice unable to contain her curiosity. "I've swallowed it" replied the March Hare. "And I've swallowed the hook, the line and the sinker that came with it."

Alice's curiosity turned to incredulity. "You swallowed the sinker? Wasn't it a bit indigestible?" "It *was* the very first time I swallowed it" replied the March Hare, "but you get used to it. It is now a part of my regular diet." Tweedledum interposed "That's my experience too." And Tweedledee agreed. "Me too" he said.

"Well" said the Mad Hatter "two people have said that the Moon is made of cheese, one has actually eaten some. Can there be any reasonable doubt here? I frankly will go further. I think that the Moon is made of the best English cheddar."

"An amendment" intervened Caterpillar. "I believe it's Wensleydale." "Cheddar" replied the Mad Hatter firmly, and Caterpillar crawled under a leaf on the table.

Alice was still unconvinced. "What about the moon-rock brought back from the moon landing.?" She asked. "American propaganda against the Russians" replied the Knave of Hearts. "The landing was filmed in the Nevada desert and that's where the rock came from."

"Well I'll eat my hat" said the Mad Hatter and promptly did so.

There was a respectful silence while this was going on.

When he finished, he asked whether the motion was agreed. "Nemine contradicente" said the White Knight. And with nobody quite knowing what that meant, they all nodded their heads including Doormouse who was still nodding away quietly under his seat.

At this point a very strange thing happened. The small black fly on the wall behind the Mad Hatter's chair suddenly took off, whizzed three times round the room at great speed, buzzing all the way. Then, Alice noticed, it suddenly turned into a wasp and stung the Mad Hatter right on the tip of his nose.

The meeting was then adjourned.

With credit to Lewis Carroll

Alan Share
3 February 2005

*i*spy – Extracts from a Blog, edited by Jan Woolf

When Alan Share commissioned me to edit his formidable 90,000 word blog - Death of a Nightingale - I thought - blimey, how can one man write so much about the SEN inclusion debate. But I was soon made aware of the passion, richness and erudition of this virtual magnum opus. Passion and well researched argument do not often go together, and what follows is a pared down, essential account of his credo around SEN which often goes to the heart of the complexities of human rights, and touches on another of his passions – music.

The two elements I especially identified with were the exposure of the corruption of much of our language around SEN, and the strong advocacy for those who are different getting what they need.

While I won't agree with all, and might argue with some of his ideas I have kept Alan's voice throughout. Most importantly, I know I'd want him on my side if I had a 'need' that was 'special' enough to warrant 'exclusion' from a world I might find threatening. Anxiety is one of the greatest barriers to learning, and Alan Share's deeply compassionate approach to children with SEN should be listened to.

Jan Woolf

Is a Detox Overdue?
April 2nd, 2009

Sometimes the words we use are the great mischief makers in our brains, setting our thoughts off on the wrong track, in the wrong direction.

We need a detox. We have to rid ourselves of toxins in our language; some of the words we use every day when we talk politics and, in particular here, special educational needs, SEN. There's also quite a bit of purging to be done elsewhere; cleaning out some of the rubbish in the corridors of power.

In this Blog I shall explore new ways of thinking and doing things.

To start, some innocent looking words that have made great mischief for years. Some words we treasure are not as innocent as they look. They have snarled up our thoughts for far too long.

I will tell you here four of them that I have in mind. You may have others. They are, in alphabetical order, "Equality"," Inclusion", "Outcomes", and "Rights." I would bin the word "Outcomes".

"Outcome' is a fine old word. 'Outcomes' is a horrid little new one. It has been designed by social engineers for social engineering. It is all about overall results that do not take account of individual needs. Travel on the London underground in the rush hour. See why it is impossible for a Whitehall civil servant to think in terms of a policy to meet individual needs. There are so many people that such a quest seems impossible. But further down the line, that is precisely what those in the public service have to do if they want to be effective, to help in any meaningful way.

Once they use the word 'outcomes' they starts to get it wrong. Those who have a mandate to govern must do so, but they must be sensitive to individual need. This is not just bourgeois self-indulgence as some may think, it is the real world.

I will mention one other toxin here. I also want to examine the pressure that people are subjected to get them to do what they don't want to do, or not do what they should. It happens today all too often in the private sector as well as the public sector.

This is a pivotal issue in my play

Is Equality Fair? Tom, Dick and Harry
April 4th, 2009

I am now going to examine the word equality. I don't think we should revere it quite as much as we do. We should use the words equity and fair play more often. You may think that equality and equity are really the same thing. Here is a story to show you that they are different.

Two friends, let's call them Tom and Dick, are on a day's walk. They encounter a third hiker, Harry, and they stop for a bite of lunch. Tom has three buns for his lunch, Dick has two, and Bill doesn't have any. Tom and Dick decide to split their buns with Harry. They cut their buns into three so that each can have five pieces. Bill is very grateful for this, and to show his thanks hands over £5 to Tom and Dick. How should this be split?

£3 to Tom and £2 to Dick? Or, £2.50 each? Neither, if you want to be strictly fair.

Consider this. The five buns have been cut into threes, making fifteen portions in all. If Bill had not come on the scene, Tom would have had nine portions, and Dick six. But when Harry comes on the scene they each take five.

Tom has lost four, Dick only one. To be fair Tom should take £4 and Dick £1.

You may prefer equality here; you may want to be generous. But equity is different. The moral of the story is that sometimes equity/fair play will be positively unequal.

But what about the legal maxim 'equity is equality'? The small step you have to take here is to accept that equity is not always equality. Sometimes it is actually unequal. The world will never look quite the same again once you have recognised the difference.

Is Equality past its sell by date?
April 5th, 2009

Equality and equality of opportunity slip off the tongue without a second thought.

But should they? Are they always the right words to use in education and in politics generally? Or are they sometimes mischief makers in the brain?

Look outside the world of education first.

We read of salaries and pensions in banking and public services. Any talk of equality there is quite ludicrous. Every day, shades of Animal Farm, we see more pigs at the trough. What makes people angry is not that those salaries not equal to their own but that there is absolutely no fairness in them.

Then there is supposed to be 'equality before the law', but is there? Can there ever be when the individual is pitched against a multi-national company or insurance company or, in a tribunal, against the State itself? I am not sure that there is even fair play. But isn't that the best you can hope for?

Translate the question into the world of health. Should taxpayers be prevented from topping up their NHS health care with medication deemed an unequal use of public funding by the National Institute of Clinical Excellence NICE? There's a double euphemism for you. Maybe you think that in the name of equality that is right, but is it fair? You see there is a difference.

Translate it into the world of annuities and car insurance premiums. The latest European dictat says that that they should be calculated without reference to the fact that women have a longer life expectancy than men – visit any care home to see this with your own eyes – and that young men have a greater risk of being involved in an accident. This flies in the face of reality in the name of equality, but it certainly isn't fair to men in the first instance and young women drivers in the second.

In education the bog-standard comprehensive school, outlawing streaming, turning polytechnics into universities and the closure of special schools all resulted from the pursuit of equality, trying to treat everyone in the same way, when they are different and have different needs.

When we talk about equality of opportunity we need to remember that one person's opportunity can be another person's roadblock. Apart from the question whether it was right to aim to get fifty per cent of school leavers into a university to get a degree pursuing the idea of equality of opportunity, what about the other fifty per cent?

People may have the same power source but they are wired differently. Accordingly, opportunities are different, and access to them should be based not on equality but on fair play in a very diverse world.

It is not even as though equality has a good provenance. Yes, racial equality. Yes, votes for all. But it provoked too much confrontation between haves and have-nots, too much revolutionary zeal in continental Europe. Too many unmarked graves.

In Britain and America fair play has been a much better, a more wholesome mantra.

Let me quote Henrietta Heald's recent biography of William Armstrong[13] that great 19th Century Northern scientist, engineer, inventor, benefactor, peer of the realm:

"He opposed the manipulation and regulation of labour in the quest for a more equal society, believing that individual ambition should be given a free rein within the law. *'Struggle for superiority is the mainspring for progress. It is an instinct deeply rooted in our nature. ... To what a dead level of mediocrity would our country sink if struggle for superiority were stamped out amongst us, and how completely would we fall back in the race of nations."*

The message that Michelle Obama, in London with Barack Obama for the G20 Meeting, delivered on her surprise visit to the girls of the Elizabeth Garrett Anderson School? *"Be the best that you can be."*

I am sorry, but those girls are not going to end up equal.

Lip service to equality in the UK has done it no favours. It has meant not so much equality of opportunity as much as equality or opportunity, not so much the pursuit of excellence as knocking excellence and pursuing mediocrity.

One of the most unfortunate consequences of this has been in relation to special educational needs. In the name of an equal right to a mainstream school, children with special needs have been denied a right to go to a special school by closing over a hundred of them.

When politicians peddle the idea of equality, I urge the old legal maxim *Caveat Emptor* – let the buyer beware - and opt for fair play instead; not a more equal society, a fairer one. That is a much, much better way of putting it.

[High flyers need to be given their chance to excel, and not just for their sake, for the country's sake as well. They could end up employing people. Those good with their hands need as much opportunity as those good with their brains. And those with special educational needs require the focused support to make sure they are not deprived of some quality in their lives. The opportunities in each case will be different.

When it comes to educational and job opportunities (as well as migrant and faith issues) fairness may sometimes be a better arbiter than equality.

Equality today is just part of a charade, the hypocrisy that we have allowed western democracy to become. Even worse than that, it leads people to knock success and excellence, a British but not an American trait, because they are so unequal.

In short it is not equality of opportunity so much as equality or opportunity.]

Where have all the Checks & Balances gone?
April 2nd, 2009

OFSTED inspects schools and Local Education Authorities. When they inspect schools they are interested in standards. When they inspect LEA's they have a totally different remit. They measure the performance of Local Authorities against nationally set targets or national averages. And standards of conduct in the process? Forget it. They're just not interested.

Local Education Authorities, knowing what is expected of them – and also what is not expected of them – will do their best to deliver, leaning on teachers and parents, with a strong bias towards inclusion that will colour consultative procedures and affect their decisions on school placements.

But what if inclusion is not all that it is cracked up to be? What if children with special needs are excluded in an inclusive environment and bullied as well? What if parents want to assert their right to have their children educated in a special school? That is what both interests and troubles me.

Shouldn't OFSTED also try to see whether LEA's meet those needs, and examine all formal complaints suggesting that they might not be doing so? This would then be part of their official report which they would be obliged to put into the public domain and which would be progressed from there.

That would at least provide some continuing check on their methods where currently there is none. And it would get away from the situation where one part of the system covers up the inadequacies of another part on the basis that 'I'll watch your back if you watch mine', dismissing well-grounded complaints as unfounded. That is the culture that actually fosters incompetence, breeds complacency and dumbs down standards. Just who is the system working for?

I would like to quote from;

Leadership by Rudolph Giuliani[10]

'The New York City school system was never really going to improve until its purpose, its core mission, was made clear. What the system should have been about was educating its million children as well as possible. **Instead, it existed to provide jobs for the people who worked in it, and to preserve those jobs regardless of performance.** *That's not to say that there weren't committed professionals at every level within the system.*

There were, and that's the shame of it. Those with their hearts in the right place were the ones who suffered most. Until I could get everyone involved to sit together and agree that the system existed to educate children, fixing little bits of it was symbolic at best. Band-aid solutions can do more harm than good. **The system needed a new philosophy. It needed to say we're not a job protection system but a system at its core about children's enrichment.** *All rewards and risks must flow from the performance of the children.'*

Self regulation clearly does not work in banking and in business generally. It does not work in the corridors of power either. In other words, start putting the checks and balances into the system one by one.

I continue my own quest for a new way of thinking, a new way of doing things and a new vocabulary, this time to suggest a way they could, but currently do not. The play enacts how James Harrington the mandarin from London, David Harding the director of education in Westborough and Gerry Thomson, special needs co-ordinator attempt to implement the policy of inclusion by pressurising the head teacher Margaret Williamson to put their case to parents. She ultimately agrees, but it takes a terrible emotional toll.

If she can't fight her corner, the governors should be able to take the issue to the Local Government Ombudsman. At the moment they are not allowed to do so.

Inclusion or Disillusion?
April 7th, 2009

I have suggested to you that you have to be very careful how you used words. If you are not careful they can be like a straight jacket. When you wear a straight jacket you can see and you can talk, but all movement is restrained. It can be the same with words. When you use them, you can see and you can speak, but your thought processes can be severely restricted. They first control what you think. They then influence what you do. Some words, like the word 'right' for instance, can change their meaning depending on how they are used.

While it may be "right" for children with special needs to go to a mainstream school they are not necessarily "wronged" if they are not. Human rights lawyers in particular please note.

Children without special needs have their rights too. Don't imagine that there cannot be a clash of interest, and one resolved by fair play rather than by Equality.

Rights! My mind goes back to a lecture by Herbert Hart, the eminent Professor of Jurisprudence at Oxford[8]. He explained that there was not one single meaning for the word 'right'. There could be five or more different meanings depending on how it was used. In addition 'rights' are not always complementary to each other and they are rarely, if ever, absolute.

Now let's look at the word 'inclusion.' Twenty years ago it was enough to say that it was all to do with equal rights – note the two words – never mind the cost, never mind the practicality. They have been teaching it and preaching it ever since. Laws passed under its influence have to be obeyed. Jobs are built around it. It is widely presumed that the Government has a policy of inclusion or an inclusion agenda.

But Baroness Warnock in a recent article, which many described as a U-turn in her position on inclusion, concluded that *'possibly the most disastrous legacy of the 1978 report was the concept of inclusion.'* She argued in the article that inclusion could be taken *'too far'* and that this was resulting in the closure of special schools to the detriment of children with SEN.

The Government has repeatedly stated that *'it is not Government policy to close special schools'* and that *'Government plays no role in relation to local authority [...] decisions to close schools.'* I am not sure that that has always been true.

But what if inclusion is not all that it is cracked up to be? What if children with special needs are excluded in an inclusive environment and bullied as well? What if parents want to assert their right to have their children educated in a special school? That is what interests me, and troubles me.

[Shouldn't OFSTED also try to see whether LEA's meet those needs, and examine all formal complaints suggesting that they might not be doing so? This would then be part of their official report which they would be obliged to put into the public domain and which would be progressed from there.

That would at least provide some continuing check on their methods where currently there is none. And it would get away from the situation where one part of the system covers up the inadequacies of another part on the basis that "I'll watch your back if you watch mine", and dismisses well-grounded complaints as unfounded. That is the culture that actually fosters incompetence, breeds complacency and dumbs down standards. Just who is the system working for?]

Can you think of any checks you would like to see on bureaucratic cock-ups? Here's another one to start you off. Should the TV programme "Watchdog" deal with some of them?

The best of lawns need the application of a weed killer as well as a feed on a regular basis. This one certainly does.

Judges[8] have ruled that children with special educational needs must receive education appropriate to those needs. All of this gives them legal protection and their legal rights – if they can exercise them. About 100 Special Schools have been closed since 1997. Parental choice? Legal rights? Tell that to the fairies.

The Ratchet Effect
April 8 2009

I have just been to the Royal Institute in Albemarle Street in London for the first time. I heard a learned discussion on how the human brain creates and appreciates Art. No-one has a clue how our brain does it! Only one of the panel of three eminent scientists and a sculptor, thought we would ever know. He was Dr. Colin Blakemore. He maintains that there is space for belief in a universal creator if you believe in such a thing, as well as the opportunity for individual humans to create if they want to. Everyone has that capacity even if they don't use it.

Another panellist, Dr. Jonathan Miller introduced me to a new thought, worked out by Michael Tomasello of the University of Leipzig. One of the things that distinguishes humans from animals is their capacity to move on with a kind of 'ratchet effect.'

Spiders are programmed to spin their intricate webs and tiny termites build their nests some 10 metres high. They are social animals, and don't just build their nests - they defend them. But that was all they could do, or had ever done. They had not advanced.

Humans, on the other hand, had the capacity to move forward, and had done so. Some humans however have all the characteristics of the termite! Political and religious bigots, for instance – and those who devise policies for special educational needs!

It's never too late to change. [however, because] We are human after all.

Bullying defeated?
April 2009

David Aaronovitch, a normally well-informed columnist, wrote in The Times on 17 March 2009 that bullying had been "defeated." Where did he get that idea?

This blog is written in cold anger, not for me but for the thousands of children with special educational needs who day after day and month after month are bullied in mainstream schools. This is not an argument against mainstream education for children with special educational needs. It is an argument for special schools as an approved alternative.

Can I quote from a report; The Bullying of Children with Learning Disabilities- ENABLE Scotland 2007[5]? [(For full report see Notes and Queries)]

'Our work with our Young People's Self Advocacy Groups has revealed that bullying is also an important issue for children and young people with learning disabilities. We joined forces with Mencap to undertake UK wide research to find out the scale and nature of the problem and most importantly to tell us more about how to stop it. We knew that bullying of children with learning disabilities existed. We knew that it is widespread and has a significant effect on children's lives. **However, we were shocked by**

the results that the survey revealed. We could not have predicted the scale of the problem, ie'

- *The sheer numbers of children who were bullied.*
- *The persistence of bullying throughout childhood.*
- *The failure of adults to stop bullying when it is reported.*
- *The range of places where bullying takes place*
- *The effects bullying has on the emotional state of children.*
- *The social exclusion faced by children who are afraid to go out.*

Bullying is not just a part of growing up. ENABLE Scotland believes that no child should have to put up with bullying and that we all have a responsibility to ensure that this stops. 93% of children with learning disabilities have been bullied 46% of children with learning disabilities have been physically assaulted. Half have been bullied persistently for more than two years.'

Now we have cyber bullying too. One parent said to me that she would gladly let an LEA official look after her son for a week so he could see what it was like, dealing with its consequences.

[You can care too much if it blinds you to uncomfortable reality. You do not see. You do not feel. Therefore you do not understand. **(Alan – I don't understand this)]**

If you haven't read William Golding's Lord of the Flies, I urge you to do so. Bullying starts in the nursery, and I am not sure that it ever stops.

We are told that the authorities know about it in schools and that they are dealing with it. They have appointed a Bullying Czar. There are school *"buddies."* And it is a learning experience kids all have got to go through. *"It is not a good reason for preferring a special school."*

If that is what you think, bully for you.

"Rights – Buttercups and daisies …
Tuesday, December 8th, 2009

.. And we are those little white dandelion heads that blow away in the wind." It is with these words that Tracey, a pupil with cystic fibrosis, introduces the audience to new version of *"Death of a Nightingale."*

Just what is the value of a right to mainstream education for children with special needs if they are then left in the hands of classroom assistants instead of trained teachers, and if they are bullied?

I quote here an article in the **Times Educational Supplement** by Kerra Maddern on 20 November 2009;

'*Teen bullying victims get two grades below the norm – Researchers claim first statistical correlation between abuse and levels of achievement.*

Bullied teenagers attain significantly lower exam results than other children, according to a study that claims to prove a statistical correlation between abuse at school and educational achievement for the first time.

The GCSE results of children bullied at 14 and 15 are two grades lower and their total score is 13 fewer points, the government-backed report says.

It also found victims of bullying were less likely to attend school full-time at 16, and that more became NEETs – not in employment, education or training. The study The Characteristics of Bullying Victims in Schools claims it is the first in-dept investigation of the impact of the problem on GCSE age pupils. Researchers studied 10,000 children; the full findings are to be published in January. Almost half of the 14 year-olds who took part said they had been bullied; this figure fell to 41 per cent at 15 and 29 per cent at 16.The most common form of bullying at all ages was name-calling and cyber bullying, followed by being threatened with violence, social exclusion and being attacked. Bullies were most likely to target those with special educational needs, young carers, pupils with a disability and children in care. Girls were more likely than boys to be bullied at age 14 and 15, although gender became less important at 16. **Previous studies have established that bullying victims have lower self-esteem and are at greater risk of suicide....**"

It is of course quite possible that the lower attainment also correlates with the extra 100,000+ teacher assistants[6] they suddenly realised they had to employ to help teachers in mainstream schools cope with the influx of children with special needs since closing 100 special schools.

The end result is, of course, the same. It matters not one iota whether lower attainment is due to bullying, the presence of teacher assistants or, most likely, a combination of both.

Faithful Infidels?
April 8 2009

We have looked at inclusion in the context of education. What about inclusion in the context of faith? I want to look at the word 'spirituality' in the context of music and faith given that they have been bedfellows since the dawn of civilisation. This is a sub plot in my book. I ask a number of questions. Mustn't we allow God some discretion as to whom He admits into his presence, not just one faith? Why do people come together in prayer only when they mourn their dead in war – and not always even then? Need religion be quite so divisive? Can we afford it to be today? Do we not now have to move on?

The question starts in our schools. Emma Kirk, the music teacher in the play is simply happy in her faith. Why can't everyone else be happy in theirs? Can she talk about it in the classroom? As one teacher put it to me when I asked her how she dealt with the very many faiths that are represented in her school in Leeds, she said *"We celebrate everything"*. Many other teachers probably do the same. That must be much better than not celebrating anything, and much more likely to lead to social cohesion. And why not some healthy scepticism too? All of this should not worry those who have true faith or real doubt.

Can we find an answer in Music?

It's where all people can come together. I call it the spiritual side of music. The spirit of God is in this music, or the human spirit. Call it either. It's the music itself, or it's the people who perform it, like you do. It's the music that some people sing to God. It's also the music they play for each other. As Emma, the music teacher says " It's the music of joy and the music of sadness. You will sense triumph over adversity and discord as well as harmony. It's the music that carries the beat of life itself. We are going to start with harmony. You see the great thing about music is that it has no boundaries."

NB A sign of the times. Just published in 2011 a new book entitled FOOD and FAITH. Christian, Jewish, Muslim, Hindu and Sikh children explain the food they enjoy as they celebrate their own faiths. Same idea.

Counting the cost
April 20th, 2009

About one hundred special schools have been closed in the past ten years. Brighouse School, the fictional setting for Death of a Nightingale, could have been one of them. Contemporary evidence suggests that if it had been, and if its pupils had been relocated in a mainstream school, many would have been bullied and their education would have suffered. Alternatively they would have ended up in another special school not designed to meet their particular needs. How did all this come about?

Some people pursuing the policy of inclusion thought that there were savings to be made. Others thought it was a matter of equality and human rights. Many probably projected what they felt in their gut what they would want for themselves onto everyone else. Also, many of those who pursued a policy of inclusion probably had no idea what a good special school was like and what it offered, and did not even know the range of special needs covered by the term Special Educational Needs.

'Brighouse School' caters for children who have physical disabilities and the learning difficulties associated with them. There are very many of these disabilities. They include cerebral palsy, spina bifida with hydrocephalus, cystic fibrosis, muscular dystrophy, rheumatoid arthritis, heart conditions, osteoagenesis imperfecta, Crohn's disease, epilepsy and neurological disorders. There are also victims of road traffic and other accidents. This is the world of burns and fractures. There are sub-divisions of each disability.

But there are also many other quite different needs and other special schools cater for them, some with a national reputation. There are children with profound and multiple learning difficulties PMLD, emotional and behavioural difficulties EBD, with hearing problems, speech or sight impairment. There is also dyslexia, dyspraxia and autism. In other words, think of a fruit shop. There are apples, pears, peaches, grapes, bananas and so on. With apples alone, there are coxes, bramleys, and golden delicious et cetera. It's the same thing with SEN. There are about 400,000 children with learning difficulties of one sort or another.

A head teacher once said to me, and the head teacher in Brighouse School echoes: "The one thing that we can give our kids is time."

Introducing Sir Humphrey Plumbton

Who is Sir Humphrey? He had a long and distinguished service with successive Conservative and Labour administrations in the Civil Service. In his retirement he published many books and papers, notably "Capitalism Without a Conscience – A Worm's Eye View", "Life in the Silo – a Study of the British Civil Service", and a training manual for politicians of all parties, entitled "Know your Place".

Some time ago I came across this extract from a report that he prepared:

I would only add one further comment on the issue of Inclusion itself.

In a paper entitled 'The Pliability of Fact in the Decision Making Process' by Vladimir Mulenchik, a Hungarian émigré who entered this country in 1956, (translated by David Hilton) and published in the late nineteen fifties, Vladimir Mulenchik pointed out that there was no absolute fact or truth in politics. There was only an illusion of it. This was as important to the world of Politics as Einstein's work on the Theory of Relativity was in relation to Physics.

It is quite facile to believe that politicians must resign every time they tell a lie. If there is no absolute truth, correspondingly there cannot be an absolute lie!

That is not what it is all about. What it is about is that there is an illusion of truth, an illusion of competence and integrity.

Ministers resign, Governments fall, Mikhail Gorbachev goes in disgrace when they shatter that illusion, when they call into question administrative competence and integrity. Sometimes, of course, it is very important that they should not resign because the resignation itself shatters that illusion. For the same reason, they should be urged not apologise for mistakes made. This is as much to protect our backs as their faces.

Let me tell you quite precisely about the greatest illusion of all in politics. It is widely thought that politicians in central and local government are served by their officials. Yes, Minister and Yes, Prime Minister gave their tacit blessing to that illusion. The sagacity and guile of Sir Humphrey regularly saved the Minister, Jim Hacker, from the dire consequences of his own simple minded and populist ineptitude.

The reality is very different. Politicians act as lightening conductors for the bolts that should fly in the direction of inept civil servants, but only very rarely strike them. I have alluded to this earlier.

That is the way of it. The illusion is reverse image of the reality. Politicians serve their officials, not the other way round. They provide the first line of defence to attack. They take the blame. They provide the safety valve for the system. Then, ultimately, if the civil service gets it wrong, they lose their seats!

We understand that from time to time MPs and Councillors have to sound off and have to appear to be supportive of the interests of their constituents, but the Whips' Offices are there to ensure that they do not overreach themselves. Patronage from 10 Downing Street is also quite a useful resource. We ought really to talk in terms of whips and carrots rather than sticks and carrots as tools of control and influence.

What is critical to that finely balanced relationship is the consistency of policy, the apparent competence of both officials and politicians and the incorruptibility of the system as a whole.

It is on the strength of that that politicians are re-elected, or not, as the case may be.

In other words, politicians come and politicians go, but we go on for ever or, at least, as long as we choose to. It is a very good system that has proved its worth over many years.

It may be subject to the criticism of inertia and insensitivity or, as the narrative alleges, myopia combined with tunnel vision, but it makes the British Civil Service the very best in the world and the envy of all democratic nations.

It is in this context that we must address the issue of Inclusion in Education.

We know full well that Inclusion is a much used, in fact over-used, word. It now means everything and nothing. But all Parties are now publicly committed to it. And some of the Governing Party's leading activists see it as an article of faith and use it as a mantra to make wholesome their egalitarian concepts. Their continuing support for the ruling party cannot be ignored, especially when other aspects of their views on egalitarianism in education have to be bypassed.

There is a limit to the number of U-turns that can be contemplated at any one time if the illusion of competence is to be sustained. We have to accept that dogma uber alles can never be an entirely alien proposition in either of the two main political parties in Britain. Pragmatism without dogma is like a ship without a rudder. That is one reason why the third party is the third party in British politics.

We have, in any event, a very clear policy to try to curtail the number of children Statemented for special education to limit its cost. We have a policy going back to the last Conservative Government when we advised them to close special schools and discourage parents from pursuing this option in the exercise of their choice for the education of their children. It ought not to be discarded, simply because its logic is now being called into question.

We are fortunate that anyone seeking to qualify Inclusion in some way is widely perceived as being an arch reactionary.

We are also fortunate that we can use, for our gospel, the UNESCO Salamanca Agreement World Statement on Special Education Needs, 1994.[3] This stated that schools are "the most effective means of combating discriminatory attitudes, creating welcoming communities, building an inclusive society and achieving education for all. Moreover, they provide an effective education to the majority of children and improve the efficiency and ultimately, the cost effectiveness of the entire education system."

This is, of course, a generalisation that totally ignores the legal imperative established by our judiciary to meet individual needs. It also ignores many consequential factors, not least costs, stress, strain, and the new word burn-out, in mainstream schools. The authors of the document actually had no evidence whatsoever for its assertion about cost effectiveness!

Furthermore, for quite a number of children with special needs, it can only reflect an aspiration rather than an expectation But it validates the policy none-the-less.

What all this means is that you do not change direction at every gust of wind, but you do have to tack into it when it blows, if you do not want your political master to capsize.

It is a pity about poor Mr. Mandelson! Civil Servants should have watched his back, even if he didn't. Unfortunately, neither he nor they studied the Training Manual "Know your Place."

For the sake of historical record, I should record that Sir Humphrey Plumbton is the highly distinguished, very eminent uncle of James Harrington, the Mandarin in my play, and is therefore my invention, as is *"The Pliability of Fact in the Decision Making Process."* Vladimir Mulenchik was the original invention of David Hilton, a very good friend in my Oxford University days, and a Liberal. Accordingly all the words above are mine, and were written a few years ago, hence the reference to Peter Mandelson.

Very sadly David died in a road accident where he was the victim. David sustained the role of Vladimir Mulenchik for two hours in a Liberal Discussion Group in Manchester with everyone throughout believing that he was none other than a Hungarian émigré. Then Liberals are very trusting people. I am very happy to dedicate this Post to his memory

Channel 4 "Born to be Different"
April 28th, 2009

Filmed over seven years, *Born to Be Different* is a frank and unsentimental portrait of the joy and heartache of life with a disabled child. Six families have allowed exceptionally intimate access to their lives following the birth of a disabled baby. The series charts everything from the initial shock of diagnosis and day-to-day practicalities, to the tough decisions and long-term reality of living with disability.

Over time, the parents' hope and fears change as they deal with medical problems, operations and the good and bad news about their child's condition – all the while trying to maintain family life.

Some families face prejudice, while others fall apart under the strain. But there are flashes of humour and the typical pleasures of childhood too. And as the children grow up, and the differences between them and their friends become more apparent, they start to articulate their own feelings.

I watched the programme last night. It told me what the head teacher of a special school told me many years ago, and that is that there are few more

caring parents than parents of children with special educational needs, as they fight to do their best for their children.

It also showed how difficult, sad, yet joyful life could be for everyone. The title, of course, underlined the fact that children with special educational needs were 'different' and that it was simplistic to a degree to think that that you could treat them all the same way - and as other children.

Life is difficult and challenging as it is, without also having to cope with seeing children bullied, and without having to deal with an unsympathetic bureaucracy working to a political agenda.

David could not tie his shoe-laces
April 30th, 2009

Music is important for all children, but especially for children with special educational needs.

Anthony Storr writes in his book *Music and the Mind*:

"David, a six-year-old autistic boy, suffered from chronic anxiety and poor visual-motor co-ordination. For nine months, efforts had been made to teach him to tie his shoe laces to no avail. However, it was discovered that his audio motor co-ordination was excellent. He could beat quite complex rhythms on a drum, and was clearly musically gifted. When a student therapist put the process of tying his shoe-laces into a song, David succeeded at the second attempt."

QUOD ERAT DEMONSTRANDUM

By the way, Emma Kirk is the music teacher in Death of a Nightingale. My own music teacher was called Mr. Kirk. I gladly dedicate the Music lessons in the play to his memory.

The World's Greatest Musical Prodigies
April 30th, 2009

Once again I was confronted by children who were "born to be different." This time they were "musical prodigies" Alexander Prior, born in London to a Russian mother and a British father and, at the advanced age of 16, a composer of no less than 40 works and a conductor, and now a third year student at the St.Petersburg Conservatory; Zhang Xiaoming, all of 10 years old from Shanghai China, and already a concert pianist; Michael Province, 13, already studying the violin for eight years, and a student at Lynn University; Simone Porter, age 12, from Seattle playing the violin with the kind of sensitivity you normally expect from someone much older; and Nathan Chan, Cello, age 15, who made his first public appearance at the age of three with the San Jose Chamber Orchestra, and is due to perform later this year with the San Francisco Symphony Orchestra.

Last night I listened to the music played by these exceptional soloists, supported by the Northern Sinfonia who must share their glow - as must Channel 4, their sponsors – as they played Beethoven, Mendelssohn, Haydn, Dvorak and the World Premier of the Concerto for Piano, 2 Violins, Cello and Orchestra 'Velesslavitsa', composed and conducted by Alexander Prior.

Standing ovations are a rare thing at the Sage Gateshead. This performance received one.

Let me also remind you of some other children, El Sistema, the youth orchestra from Venezuela and its conductor Gustavo Dudamel. These children were not born to be different, but have become so. Let me quote Ed Vulliami in the Observer on 29th July 2007.

This is more than the story of one prodigy, himself from a poor family on the outskirts of Barquisimeto in the Venezuelan interior. This is about what Dudamel calls 'music as social saviour'. He and his orchestra are but the apex of a unique enterprise; the zenith of something deeply rooted in Venezuela, formally entitled the National System of Youth and Children's Orchestras of Venezuela, but known simply as El Sistema.

Inspired and founded in 1975 under the slogan *'play and fight!'* by the extraordinary social crusader Jose Antonio Abreu, El Sistema flourished with a simple dictum: that in the poorest slums of the world, with the pitfalls of drug addiction, crime and despair, life can be changed and fulfilled if children can be brought into an orchestra. The road taken by Dudamel and his orchestra is one along which some 270,000 young Venezuelans are now registered to aspire, playing music across a land seeded with 220 youth orchestras from the Andes to the Caribbean. Sir Simon Rattle, music director of the mighty Berlin Philharmonic, describes El Sistema as *'nothing less than a miracle... From here, I see the future of music for the whole world.'* But, adds Sir Simon, *'I see this programme not only as a question of art, but deep down as a social initiative. It has saved many lives, and will continue to save them.'*

Across Venezuela, young barrio-dwellers spend their afternoons practising Beethoven and Brahms. They learn the *'Trauermarsch'* from Mahler's fifth symphony. Teenagers like Renee Arias, practising Bizet's Carmen Suite at a home for abandoned and abused children, who, when asked what he would be doing if he had not taken up the French horn, replies straightforwardly: *'I'd be where I was, only further down the line – either dead or still living on the streets smoking crack, like when I was eight.'* Or children like Aluisa Patino, 11, who states plainly that she learns the viola *'to get myself and my mother out of the barrio.'*

So, music is not just for the gifted, nor just for the affluent. It is music for everyone. It is where inclusion really works; but it comes up from the ground, it is not imposed; and it sits alongside a quest for excellence and an acceptance of discipline. That was the message that Gustavo Dudamel and Jose Antonio Abreu delivered in a recent Symposium at the South Bank Centre after their orchestra's trail blazing and quite spectacular performance there.

I was at a concert last week, given by the country's National Youth Orchestra, 175 strong. **Let me quote one of them, Abigail Gostick, a clarinetist from Newbury, age 17:**

"Although I am still deciding upon my next steps within the world of music, the NYO has opened up a world of possibilities. This summer, I was lucky enough to be among a small group of NYO musicians working for a week with children who have physical disabilities at a school in Hampshire. It was amazing and deeply rewarding to watch the smiles on their faces as they heard live instruments for the first time and then had the opportunity to lead the ensemble themselves using speech and body movement. To know you can have that kind of impact on people with music is incredibly inspiring. The week has helped me to appreciate that not everyone has the ability to communicate as easily as we do but through the 'universal language' of music, we are able to connect with and bring out the best in people."

Look, listen and learn.

An Abattoir for Sacred Cows
May 9th, 2009

The Department of Health White Paper - *Valuing People* envisages an annual increase of around one per cent of children with severe learning difficulties. If their parents want them to be educated in a special school, they need to receive a Statement. Statementing is a bureaucratic process under the control of Local Education Authorities (LEAs). It could be, and it should be a multidisciplinary one, but it isn't. It is regulated by Law and is designed to define the very different needs of children requiring special attention and the way those needs are to be met. It is a passport to admission to a special school that is impossible without it.

There is a fiction – and it really is a fiction – that tribunals are not the same as courts. *It is suggested that they are just informal proceedings with the law absent, and that lawyers are superfluous and independent. I am sorry to disillusion you. The Law is ever present. Statutes, Statutory Orders and the precedent of previous cases guide decision taking, although these can sometimes be total gobbledegook to the layperson. Witnesses present evidence, but need to have their arguments questioned in cross-examination. A paid lawyer, who is appointed by the Lord Chancellor, acts as chair of the panel. Members are appointed by the DfES. There are 175 such Tribunals throughout the country.*

The scales are weighted against parents. *Criminals are entitled to legal aid defence, but this is not the case with parents of children with special needs trying to do their best for their children, and, they may have to pay for a lawyer if they want one. Furthermore, if they have to get medical reports, they have to pay for those too.*

The answer is not to provide legal aid in the present economic climate. There could, I suggest, be a 'pro bono' role for 3rd year students in the law departments of universities, a useful learning experience – maybe better than studying Roman law – and much better than nothing for parents.

Better still slay two sacred cows instead.

- **Sacred Cow Number One: the writing of Statements by civil servants. End it.**

- **Sacred Cow Number Two: scrap Special Educational Needs tribunals, with all the paper-chasing, time consuming, and money-wasting rigmarole** that they involve.

Why not appoint multi-disciplinary bodies, comprising retired head teachers, medics, physio's, educational psychologists and one or two lay members to work off reports, and draw up Statements of Educational Need? A clerk could keep them right by the law. Then, if parents do not go along with their decision, give them a personal hearing and pay for any evidence they want to provide.

Sorry. There will be no jobs for the boys ... or girls, no jobs for lawyers or accountants. But it should save some money.

Another Bite into a Wormy Apple
May 13th, 2009

Here I give you the first and, so far as I am concerned, the last law of good civil administration: Those who serve the public should be fully accountable to the public. *I have already suggested that OFSTED should examine the handling of all formal complaints against LEAs, making this part of their official report, and be obliged to put it into the public domain. I have also urged that the TV programme "Watchdog" should expose administrative cock-ups.*

We have an Ombudsman positioned to provide the citizen with a check on the abuse of power by the civil service. As matters stand those serving on public bodies such as Boards of Governors have no right of access with a complaint unless they can show personal loss. Informed whistleblowers keep out!

Here is another suggestion. Empower the Ombudsman to take all complaints from any UK citizen against State mismanagement or malpractice when all other forms of complaint have been exhausted, and again put the report into the public domain.

MPs are currently being shamed into putting their house in order. It is high time that the civil service was also shamed into putting its house in order in every tier of government.

The Iron Fist In A Velvet Glove
May 25th, 2009

In this Post I am going to write about money and power. *People get upset about the "money" side of capitalism, especially clerics. They should be more concerned about the abuse of power, the power that money brings; it is also the power that communism, socialism, yes even our democracy brings. And when I talk about the abuse of power, I am talking about power over people, religious as well as secular, commercial as well as political.*

Power does not exist in a vacuum.

As Justice Brandeis has warned:

'Experience should teach us to be most on our guard when the government's purposes are beneficent. Men born to freedom are naturally alert to repel invasion of their liberty by evil-minded rulers. The greatest dangers to liberty lurk in insidious encroachment by men of zeal, well-meaning, but without understanding.'

'The first task of a society that would have liberty and privacy is to guard against the misuse of physical coercion on the part of the state and private parties. The second task is to guard against the softer forms of secret and manipulative control. Because they are subtle, indirect, invisible, diffuse, deceptive, and shrouded in benign justifications, this is clearly the more difficult task'. **[Olmstead, 1927]**

What is important to understand is not just how power is used or misused, but our increasing vulnerability to it.

Many people are directly employed by the State and will retain or enhance that employment by being subservient to it. Many are not employed by the State but owe their livelihood to it. Lawyers get briefs. They aspire to become QCs or judges – state appointments. Leading firms of accountants and Academia get millions of pounds worth of consultation work from Departments of State. None of them will want to be too argumentative or too 'independent.' All have families to feed, and a comfortable retirement to look forward to.

Beyond that, the State controls where children are educated as well as the medicines that we are entitled to. It now has a stake in our banks and building societies that control our money supply.

It should not be altogether surprising that there are all those working in the public sector who feel obliged to do some things they know they shouldn't be doing, or not do things that they should. There are school governors, and people like them, who are doing valuable voluntary work within the community, but who are deliberately denied the tools to do it properly by those who prefer to do it themselves, but want to make it look otherwise.

It is the System that needs looking at, the con in consultation, the charade of partnership.

Here's one small suggestion.

Shouldn't the school governors be involved in writing the references for a head teacher, not just the local educational authority? Surely no-one knows the head teacher better. This would be just a tiny change that could help to free up head teachers to be true to themselves and not slaves to a system. I hope that this helps you to see what I am getting at.

Can you think of any other small things that would help to empower people?

Remember, a game of chess consists of many small moves, the largest wall many tiny bricks

Like Hitting a Rolled-up Sock.
June 14th, 2009

A golfing friend of mine uses these words to describe a bad golf shot where the ball doesn't travel very far. This is what it can be like when you try to fight the System.

Unfortunately the people who just want to build and defend their own nests – I call them 'termites' - are everywhere. They populate Parliament, local and central Government, the learned professions, academia, the unions, banking and commerce - united by one simple notion 'You watch my back and I'll watch yours.'

This forms the System!

Let me cite an experience outside my dealings with central and local government.

Many years ago I chaired an Action Committee in the UK Furniture and Carpet Industry, representing leading manufacturers and retailers. It was formed in response to Government criticisms of the Industry, in particular its failure to offer the consumer a quality product and quality service. Out of this was born the Qualitas Conciliation Service, (now the Furniture Ombudsman.)

But we came up with a bigger package than that. It required all upholstery to be tested for performance. It required a labeling scheme complete with icons to advise the consumer how to select and use their furniture.

When the Government of the day removed the threat of legislative intervention, the termites in the industry and its Trade Association took over. And nothing came of it. They said they cared. Some did. Most didn't. And many of them have gone out of business since. They thought the bottom line was one year's net profit.

The very bottom line is whether a company meets its customers' needs – or not.

Those who have read earlier Posts will recognise this. The importance of meeting individual needs is a familiar theme.

Let me describe another experience. I chair a care home for the elderly. They are regularly inspected by the authorities. The staff happen to be very good anyway, legitimately wearing the badge of excellence that they have been awarded. But these inspections keep them on their toes, the unannounced ones especially so. There are no termites in this care home as a result.

Sometimes the System does get it right. It should do so more often.

Another Fine Mess
June 17 2009

The BBC (16 June 2009) reports concern over school medical care.

'Schools are putting teaching assistants under increasing pressure to carry out medical procedures without appropriate training, a union warns. Unison says most support staff only hold a basic first aid certificate. But some are being asked to carry out procedures such as administering drugs for heart problems, changing colostomy bags and testing blood sugar levels.'

"Imagine the pressure of being told that a child could not go on a trip unless you would change their colostomy bag" Christina McAnea Unison.

Government guidelines say staff must be properly trained before carrying out any medical procedure. They stress that it is the responsibility of schools to make sure that is happening. Unison is calling for the introduction of new, tougher guidelines setting out what support staff should and should not be asked to do. The survey found 85% of the 334 respondents were expected to provide medical support, and 70% to administer medicines as part of their job – even though these are voluntary duties.

Michelle McKenna, a school support worker, *"it is only a matter of time before something terrible happens".*

One in four respondents did not feel competent and comfortable with the responsibility of administering medicines or providing medical support. And one in three said they were not familiar with school policy on how to do it.

Put very simply, carers are not nurses, and in a care home as against a nursing home, only qualified district nurses can legally undertake nursing procedures. I can't believe that the same should not apply in our schools. Care assistants have their rights too.

Local Authorities have a duty of care laid down in a case in the highest Court in the land, the House of Lords, when four of them tried unsuccessfully to disown it.[8]

The picture gets worse. Here are some extracts from Education Policy Partnership, December 2003 Review – The impact of paid adult support on the participation and learning of pupils in mainstream schools

A recent government consultation paper on the role of school support staff DfES, 2002 indicated that there were over 100,000 working in schools – an increase of over 50 percent since 1997. I quote from the report.

- *Paid adult support staff can sometimes be seen as stigmatising the pupils they support. Paid adult support staff can sometimes thwart inclusion by working in relative isolation with the pupils they are supporting and by not helping their pupils, other pupils in the class and the classroom teacher to interact with each other.*
- *Paid adult support shows no consistent or clear overall effect on class attainment scores. Paid adult support may have an impact on individual but not class test scores.*
- *Most significantly, there is evidence from several studies of a tension between paid adult support staff behaviour that contributes to short-term changes in pupils, and those which are associated with the longer-term development of pupils as learners. Paid adult support strategies associated with on-task behaviour in the short term do not necessarily help pupils to construct their own identity as learners, and some studies in this cluster suggest that in such strategies can actively hinder this process.*
- *Paid adult support staff can positively affect on-task behaviour of students through their close proximity. Continuous close proximity of paid adult support can have unintended, negative effects on longer-term aspects of pupil participation and teacher engagement. Less engaged teachers can be associated with the isolation of both students with disabilities and their support staff, insular relationships between paid adult support staff and students, and stigmatisation of pupils who come to reject the close proximity of paid adult support.*
- *Given current interest in involving users in planning, carrying out and evaluating research, it is surprising that so few studies actually focus on the pupils' views.*

This is every bit as damning as the BBC Report.

And here are a couple of extracts from a piece of research from the Research Unit of Newcastle University. They explain absolutely everything, even though it may not be what its authors intended. Please note the year. The policy was well under way by then.

8 Extracts from Costs and Outcomes for Pupils with Moderate Learning Difficulties in Special and Mainstream Schools 1999[4]

p 14 *We have some generalised findings on outcomes from our literature survey and these are highly suggestive – but they do not make it possible to evaluate the cost-effectiveness of the schools in our study,…..For many, inclusion is a fundamental human right – not simply one form of SEN provision amongst many, to be evaluated on the balance of advantage it confers on children. It is important to be clear, therefore, that an analysis of costs and outcomes cannot properly be used to determine questions of rights.*

P71 *The state of our knowledge about outcomes for pupils with MLD is not good, and our understanding of the relationship between costs and outcomes is even worse.*

For those who imagine that the policy of Inclusion saves taxpayers' money please note that one classroom assistant costs more than the entire cost of a pupil's education in a special school.

(There are now over 200,000 non-teaching care assistants. A recent report from the Sutton Trust[6] says that they are not good value for money.)

Annabelle's Holiday
June 23rd, 2009

In this Post I invite you to think about the role of the private benefactor.

There are some on the Left who see the State as the great provider and they marginalise as intruders those individuals who try to make a contribution. Meanwhile, some on the Right satisfy their consciences when they leave it to the State to look after those less fortunate than themselves.

In the UK, when we can anticipate a leaner, meaner State, with £175 billion of debt to support, it is worth asking whether either of these attitudes makes sense. **A very generous donation of £1,000 to the "Death of a Nightingale Fund" brings me to Annabelle, to her mother and her younger sister. The donation, made up to £1,500 from the Fund, has enabled the whole family, with Annabelle's helper, afford a holiday in London.**

The interesting fact here is that the State generally has been very supportive of the family. It is life itself that has been unfair.

Annabelle's mum has been the heroine. Both she and her sister had cancer early in their lives; she was diagnosed at the age of 19, her sister at the age of 25. Her sister died of it in 1997, leaving a young child.

She had the agony of deciding whether to have both or one of her ovaries removed, and has now lost both. Before that, in April 1998, she gave birth to Annabelle only to discover after a while that she was severely disabled. Meanwhile in July 1999 she gave birth to Elizabeth. Shortly after this her partner left her to fend for herself withdrawing his financial support.

There is no complaint here against the NHS, only gratitude. Social Services provide a carer for a couple of hours a week to help her to be more inclusive in the community and to spend quality time with Elizabeth. Bullying is not, as I understand it, an issue as it is unfortunately with many children and their parents, nor has there been the misplaced insensitivity of hard hearted officialdom. Life itself has been its own taskmaster.

I have met many mums like Annabelle's and some dads too. When they had children with special educational needs – sometimes more than one – they could share their love equally, but not their time. Here fairness was the only measure, and not always easy to come by: there is a moral in that. These were the kind of people I was pleased to be able to help save their schools from closure.

It is in that context [that I have already suggested] that deprivation should be of greater concern than disability. With the aid of time, patience and professional help - and you need all three - you can work your way around a disability, and learn to live with it. In many cases these children need time and patience. They need dedicated teachers, carers, school nurses, physio's, speech and language therapists and others who have the expertise to give them the one chance that they have to find their place in the world. This is what a good special school can provide.

Deprivation is another matter.

A holiday, even in the UK, for a family with a disabled youngster is always going to be more difficult to plan, more expensive too. It is a real loss if it is out of reach especially when everyone else is showing off their holiday snapshots.

It is most unlikely that the State is going to help here. Hence the opportunity for you to get some real satisfaction that comes from personally lending a helping hand.

The Purse Strings of Power
July 22nd, 2009

I am going to write about money. You can't get very far without it. The way that it is handled, from the Treasury downwards, has to be a very powerful management tool. It has been a powerful force implementing the policy of inclusion. As the 'good book' says "The Lord giveth and the Lord taketh away."

Don't underestimate the role of the Treasury. "Death of a Nightingale" explores the area where control should stop and participation begin. As you read what follows you may wonder whether the one does stop and whether the other actually does begin.

These are just some of the proposals I made as a governor in 2004.

* *The Budget approved by the Governing Body should be included in or attached to the minutes of the meeting where it is agreed. The Budget should anticipate all anticipated income and expenditure, capital and revenue, affecting the School for the year in question.*
* *No changes should be made to the budget without the agreement of Governing Body recorded in the minutes.*
* *Indicative Budgets should always be presented to the Finance Sub-Committee and then the Governing Body, as well as to head teachers, in time for its contents to be questioned and, if necessary, amended. It should be presented alongside the budget and the performance up date for the current year.*
* *The Finance Committee should review - at least termly- the capital and revenue income and expenditure accounts compared against budget and previous year's spend with a note of variance at the time. The variance should not be variance against total budget spend for the year as a whole. Any variance of more than say 5% shall be reported to the termly meeting of the Governing Body.*
* *A system of accruals that is the norm in business accounting should be adopted as soon as possible.*

Should I have had to recommend these things? The setting and monitoring of budgets is key to any enterprise. It should be the easiest thing in the world to organise. It is, after all, simply money IN and money OUT. In my working life I have been involved with many budgets, but as a governor I actually had to ask a chartered accountant to explain to me how the LEA had put its figures together.

Does the Treasury really want to encourage participation? Do they? Does anyone?

Over the years I have come across many very worthy charities from bereavement counseling to work with deprived families. Every year each one of them goes out with a begging bowl just to survive. Professional carers have to spend their valuable time trying to raise money. They all had one thing in common. They had no core funding. Larger charities have no such problem, and they don't worry about it.

This situation is going to get worse not better as public expenditure is cut, and the nation feels itself poorer and needs become greater.

Around the country Community Foundations help donors identify well run charities to which their charitable donations can be given and they make a genuine difference to people's lives. They have grown rapidly in recent years. There are now 55 of them, and they can reach 95% of the UK's population. They already make grants of about £70m every year. The State should provide these Foundations with matched funding to enable them to allocate core funding to selected charities.

It is going to become increasingly evident that the State does not have the resources to make necessary social provision on its own. **Social provision should be seen as a working partnership between the State and charities, and the State needs to put its money where its mouth is. It says that it cares.**

"Make money work better" would be a good mission statement, especially in times of financial stringency. This would be one sure way.

Likewise running schools needs to be seen as a working partnership between the State and Governors who give their time and their know how without payment.

Will they stop the pretence that they are creating partnerships and will they actively encourage participation? I wonder.

Parent Power, its Strengths and Weakness
August 16th, 2009

Children with special needs. Do not forget their parents. They too have their rights. And they have very real responsibilities that they feel more than most, and they *fight for their children's wellbeing. They care. They really do. When 'my' school was threatened with closure, its head teacher at the time said to me that the Local Authority trying to close the school would have to deal with that. They never quite did, and the school is still there to this day.*

Death of a Nightingale is not about that school. It is more about the 100 special schools that have been closed in the UK since 1997. It is a work of fiction, but every now and again the facts of my own experience come to the surface. I can never forget them.

The moral of this particular post is very simple. If you want to help children with special needs don't just project your own needs as you see them or imagine them on to everyone else. Their needs may be different. And don't just work it out in 'the library of your mind.'

Don't be reassured by those who say that inclusion is working or will work with a little more money and training, when politically they can't say what they really think. The facts are otherwise. [Read Baroness Warnock.] **Think of the individual child. Teachers, carers and therapists have to. And think of their parents, too. They are in the frame not outside it.**

A Glaring Omission – but why?
February 2010

Let me explain.

Newcastle University is currently presenting a number of public lectures in the Curtis Auditorium under the banner of INSIGHTS. Sir Martin Harris gave the first of them this week on "Excellence and Inclusion in Higher Education." *Sir Martin is a heavyweight. Amongst* *other things formerly Manchester University vice chancellor and then Vice Chancellor of the University of Salford, but here as the Director of Fair Access to Higher Education.*

There was a lot about Sir Martin's lecture that I applauded. He espoused the pursuit of excellence. He endorsed meritocracy. He drew a distinction between excellence - which he favoured - and elitism which he disapproved of. He assured his audience that universities had to remain one hundred per cent in charge of admissions. Not a teeny weeny bit of pressure to admit more students from working class backgrounds? No positive discrimination in favour of some that becomes actual discrimination against others, such as all-women MP shortlists under Harriet Harman's banner of equality? Well I wonder, but never mind. *Of course he saw his remit as the pursuit of 'equality of opportunity.'*

What was quite startling to me was that in a fifty minute lecture on a subject with the word "Inclusion" in its title, from first to last he never once mentioned inclusion for students with special educational needs. It is interesting when you come to think about it; I have read a lot about inclusion of children with special needs into mainstream schools over the years but I have seen nothing that I can recall about its provision in Higher Education. Not once.

You would have thought that someone who was a Director of Fair Access to Universities would have this within his remit. This is where inclusion ought really to click in for those who have survived the bullying, overcome their learning difficulties and started to embark on their adult lives.

This is where I fully endorse it, but where the educational establishment and academia would appear totally to ignore it. Ah well. Maybe they thought, quite mistakenly as it happens, that inclusion would save money, but here they knew it would cost money in terms of access and support. Perhaps they didn't even acknowledge that there would be some children with special needs that would aspire to higher education. Perhaps it was providing them with unequal support.

By strange coincidence part of a BBC report states figures from the Student Loans Company showing that 12,500 students in England are still waiting for grants to pay for specialist equipment. The statistics also reveal that two thirds of students with a disability or special needs are still waiting for money.

Listening to the Deaf
April 4 2010

And here's some more sad news that has just come my way – in an **angry statement from the NDCS (National Deaf Children's Society)**

'In a debate on the Equality Bill in the House of Lords on 27th January, the Government refused to take action that would help ensure a fair and equitable exam system for disabled students. NDCS is deeply concerned that the current drafting of the Bill will allow exam bodies to discriminate against disabled students. Jo Campion, Head of Campaigns at NDCS, said

'The Equality Bill was meant to remove all traces of discrimination in exams, but instead maintains a system which is unfairly loaded against disabled students. It now enables a range of unnecessary get-out clauses for exam bodies to avoid having to make exams genuinely accessible.'

Government figures show that deaf children are already under achieving at school. These new laws will make it even harder for deaf children to get the qualifications they need to be independent and successful in life. Deaf students and their parents will be expressing anger and disappointment today that the Government has sided with exam bodies rather than disabled students. In 2005, the exams regulator withdrew support available to disabled candidates. NDCS successfully fought to get this support reinstated for deaf students, however NDCS continues to receive complaints from deaf students and parents highlighting that this support is not being provided.

NDCS is calling on the Government to urgently reconsider its position and ensure the Equality Bill provides genuine access to examinations for disabled students. Deaf students currently experience the following examples of discrimination; failure to provide written transcripts for video or radio recordings, failure to provide extra time to lip-read instructions and being asked questions which are inappropriate for a deaf young person to answer. For example, a deaf student was asked in an English exam to describe how it felt to be a fan of a music band. The examining body refused to accept that the question would disadvantage a student who has no experience of listening to music.

The State is falling down on both counts – equality and fair play.

The Pursuit of Excellence - SHOCK TREATMENT!
May 25th, 2010

Some things sadden me. Some things appall me. In a comment on my last post *Crina wrote "But I believe the point I failed to make was that excellence will always be a minority, because most people are not interested in promoting it." This saddens me. It should worry you.*

David Gale wrote "The words of our local Director of Children's Services still ring in my ears, "Gifted children are excluded from our Inclusion Strategy". This appalls me.

Chris Woodhead wrote in his weekly column in the Sunday Times, "Earlier this year ministers decided to stop funding the gifted and talented programme in order to divert funds to the 'disadvantaged." This also appalls me.

Recently a retired teacher said to me that one reason why girls were doing better than boys today was that boys ridiculed those in their class who were "swots".

The following was a part of OFSTED's glowing report on the special school that I was a governor of for many years. "...a good school with many outstanding features... pupils in the school are highly motivated, eager to learn and responsive to the high expectations of their teachers.... the School's ethos is very positive." It didn't stop the local authority wanting to close it. The parents successfully fought to keep it open.

But over a 100 special schools were closed, many of them I am sure just as excellent.

Some people actually begrudge excellence, are jealous of it. They label it as elitism when it is nothing of the sort.

This post is written for the benefit of all those who think that the pursuit of excellence is either a complete waste of time or positively wrong because it makes society less equal.

Academies - A Hot Air Balloon?
July 11th, 2010

Hansard 7 July 2010:

Q7. [6252] **Mr Robert Buckland (South Swindon) (Con):** *Will my right hon. friend give an assurance that all new academies that will be set up will be obliged to accept children with special educational needs?*

The Prime Minister: *I can absolutely give my hon. friend that assurance. Academies will be required to ensure that pupils with special educational needs are admitted on the same basis as other schools. Children with special educational needs have special needs, and a compassionate, decent and tolerant country will ensure that they get the help, support, education and love that they need.*

Do these words reassure you? Do they ring true in the real world outside Parliament? Do they ring true in the classrooms of the real world outside cloistered academia?

Let me remind you what the law [8] **states that society must provide:**

Clause 1 (3), 2001 SEN Act: *'If a statement is maintained under section 324 for the child, he must be educated in a mainstream school unless that is incompatible with – (a) the wishes of his parent, or (b) the provision of efficient education for other children.'*

[Catchpole v Buckingham County Council and another, *'The Times Law Reports on 18 March 1999,]* Lord Justice Thorpe [said] "the local education authority had a duty to ensure that a child with special education needs was placed at a school that was appropriate. It was not enough for the school to be merely adequate."*

[Phelps v Hillingdon Borough Council, Anderton v Clwyd County Council, Gower v Bromley London Borough Council and Jarvis v Hampshire Country Council.] *Times Law Reports,* July 28,2000. The House of Lords ruled that LEA's duty of care required them to *'have to take reasonable care of their health and safety including the monitoring of their needs and performance.'*

Here are some questions someone might care to put to the Prime Minister.

1. Yes, Academies will admit children with special needs, but will they provide education that is appropriate to the needs of children with special needs? Will they have ring-fenced funding? Will trained professionals be around with time to give them? And will this be done without prejudicing the rights of children without special needs to receive education that is appropriate to them?
2. Will other mainstream schools in a period of austerity be able to meet those needs?
3. And the question those wedded to the dogma of inclusion never think about asking, do they? If parents find that the needs of their children are not being met in mainstream schools and want to assert their statutory right to opt out of them, will there be special schools around that can provide that '*appropriate*' provision that they can opt into?

[57] A TALE OF TWO RIGHTS – NOT JUST ONE!
July 24th, 2010

I do not normally read law reports in The Times. But on the 15 July this year the headline "Delay did not deny right to education" caught my eye. But in this instance the delay did! The Times got it wrong.

The case: A v Essex County Council

When I read it, I saw that it was about the rights of an autistic child and they were being argued out in the Supreme Court. It must have been a close run thing because the decision voiced by Lord Phillips was a majority decision, three to two. The decision was against the child.

I felt for the child and for the local authority. The educational needs of the one, and the difficulty meeting those needs of the other. It was a very sad situation. I felt for the Court too.

The child, named A, was autistic with a severe learning disability. He also had a severe communication disorder and challenging behaviour. He suffered from epilepsy; frequently having 10 to 15 short epileptic fits a day, despite medication. He was doubly incontinent, had no concept of danger and required constant supervision.

At the age of 12 he was excluded from his school because it couldn't cope. It took eighteen months to assess his needs and find residential accommodation for him. The case was all about those eighteen months. Had he been deprived of the education he was entitled to during that time?

As I read the heading to The Times law report, I realised that the case was wrongly described. Shame on The Times! It should not have read 'Delay did not deny right to education.' It should have read, "Delay denied the right to special school". The 'right' to education was only to a mainstream school. It was not disputed that child A could not exercise it, having been excluded.

What about the right to opt out?

These were the words that Lord Phillips used:

"The authorities ... did not support the proposition that article 2 imposed ... a positive obligation to provide education that catered for the special needs of the small, if significant portion of the population which was unable to profit from mainstream education.... The right of access to education conferred on A had to have regard to the limited resources actually available to deal with his special needs."

WOW, as they say. Brothers, sisters, comrades and all you lawyers and academics trumpeting 'rights' provided by Parliament or, better still, in the European Convention of Human Rights, it is high time you realised that sometimes rights are worth no more than the pot of gold buried at the end of a rainbow, and just when you most need them.

Let me underline what precisely this means in the context of special educational needs.

Over 100 special schools were closed from 1997 onwards. *'For a small if significant portion of the population'* this curtailed those resources. So, for some children it actually destroyed the 'right to education' enshrined in article 2 of Protocol 1 of the European Convention of Human Rights. In the future, parents wanting their children educated in a special school will find this case argued as a precedent against them.

I do not criticise the judges for seeing the world as it is, not just as they would like it to be. They are not the problem. I do criticise the politicians, lawyers and academics – those who fashion and lead opinion – the social engineers among them. They never seem to take into account how the world actually is when they try to make it how they would like it to be, totally ignoring human frailty. I especially criticise those who *'delete without reading'* anything that conflicts with their mind set opinions. They are the real termites.

Just what is the value of a right to mainstream education for children with special needs if they are then left in the hands of classroom assistants ('amiable mums' as they are affectionately called) instead of trained teachers with time to give them. And if they are bullied? What about the right to opt out?

I have seen a boy controlling his computer with a wand attached to his forehead in a special school. I have seen children rescued from bullying in mainstream schools. I have listened to their parents. For them it was not just a 'learning experience.'

When so many special schools have been closed, when resources are tight, when all the talk is about voluntary effort and the tiny question that has to be asked, apart from any other, is where it is going to get its core funding from, just how do we make sure that children with special needs receive the skilled professional support that they need?

AN OPEN LETTER TO SARAH TEATHER

Date? Can you provide one?

This post is an open letter to Sarah Teather, LibDem MP, Minister of State for Children and Families

Dear Minister

A few years ago when you were in Opposition you wrote to me saying that the shortcomings of Inclusion in relation to Special Educational Needs should be addressed by an increase in funding.

If this was right – but I don't think that it was – then you have a real problem this autumn when you issue a Green Paper with your proposals for SEN.

There is, of course, nothing like real power and responsibility as Minister of State for Children and Families to bring home the truth of a situation. The evidence is now piling up that inclusion was a disaster in the making.

Its shortcomings had nothing whatsoever to do with money. The Labour Government threw money at it like confetti, trying to make it work; it recruited a paper-led army to run it. It was a flagship policy, all complete with target practice under the supervision of OFSTED. But you heard less and less of the word 'inclusion' as time went by, and the flagship was taken out of the line altogether during the last general election.

Putting it quite simply, it was a cock-up by everyone.

The Treasury, advised by accountants Coopers & Lybrand, thought that there were savings to be made by including children with special needs in mainstream instead of special schools. It never occurred to them that mainstream schools would have to employ about 100,000 classroom assistants (now over 200,000[6]) at about £15k a time to help them cope with the influx after the closure of 100 special schools. Job creation certainly. Cost to the taxpayer a matter of no consequence. There is never a shortage of people living in "wouldn't-it-be-nice-if" land, and especially in the world of education.

That is not to say that more children with special needs should not be admitted to mainstream schools; that provision should not be made for them there. There will always be winners in the lottery of life; but there are losers too unless you are careful,

What I find necessary to keep saying is that there should always be a choice between mainstream and special schools. As I said in my last post, "Yes" a right to a mainstream education with some sensible caveats. But "Yes" also a right to opt out of mainstream schools to a special school, again with sensible caveats. Neither of these rights can guarantee education appropriate to individual need, but at least they can try to. Don't be satisfied if it is merely adequate. The Law is not satisfied. You should not be either.

So, when you prepare your Green Paper this autumn I suggest that you start with two blank pieces of paper.

On one of them write what you want to achieve, and on the other how you propose to achieve it.

What you should want to achieve is very simple – meeting the extremely diverse needs of children with special educational needs.

That should be paramount. I know there are those who think it is a bourgeois fad to assert individual need, but maybe they don't have children with special needs themselves or have not taught them.

As you develop your mission statement avoid all words to do with "social engineering", words like "inclusion", "outcomes" and, yes, "equality of opportunity" too. Children don't want to be social experiments. They only have one chance.

Adopt instead "value-added" words like "excellence", "opportunity", "fair play". These words will measure the success of your policy.

On the other piece of paper write the words "professionalism and commitment by those who care".

As you develop these words recognise that local education authorities are not best placed to handle special education on a day-to-day basis. Their boundaries are too small. Their responsibilities are too diffuse, and the financial and political constraints under which they work get in the way. Too often they can't afford to care.

I know that there are many in Local Government who mean well but they, like everyone else, end up as casualties of a bureaucratic system that constantly short-changes children.

It is important that you grasp WHY?

Let me illustrate what I am saying. Little Johnny is blind. There is a school for the blind outside his local authority area. The local authority will not want the cost of sending him there, and little Johnny's parents will have a battle on their hands, But there actually isn't a school for the blind in a neighbouring authority because the catchment area of a single local authority is not big enough to support one. It is a CATCH 22 situation.

I urge you not to under-value professionalism and ignore commitment. When dealing with children with special needs you need both. Mainstream schools often dilute them. That is the price you pay when you rely on classroom assistants – "amiable mums" as they are called – to do the work of professional teachers and therapists.

What do I mean by "professionalism"? A potent mix of talent, self discipline, training, practice over many years, an exquisite care for detail, sorry no nine to five stuff, and preferably no skullduggery. The only way we can properly claim that the British are "the best" at anything in the world is if we start to reassert this.

And what do I mean by "commitment"? Simply service above self.

You really need both of them in all walks of life.

I know that Michael Gove is opening the door to parents to create their own schools. Parents of children with special needs have their work cut out just looking after and bringing up their children without opening schools for them.

If you can establish a strategic partnership with Disability Organisations, and structure a way to harness their knowhow and their concern with a new range of community schools with pooled resources for children with special needs, you can make this a part of your Big Society.

In short, dump "Inclusion" as a watchword and substitute the words "Excellence and Opportunity." These are the words that should flower in your garden. In my experience they have less to do with money and more to do with attitude of mind.

You might get somewhere if the Coalition asserted these words elsewhere as well, and you didn't just talk interminably of "austerity" and "financial cuts".

Yours sincerely
Alan Share

I have received a reply. I quote these paragraphs:

'As you are aware, we will launch a Green Paper in the autumn to look at a wide range of issues for children with SEN and disabilities. Before then we will be looking at the results of the Ofsted review of SEN we are expecting later this summer, in addition to the many reviews of SEN policy

in recent years. We will also be listening to the views of parents, teachers and organisations with an interest in this area.

'We'll be looking at things like parental choice. This will mean looking at ending the bias towards mainstreaming, but that does not mean limiting mainstream provision for children with SEN and disabilities. It's about recognising that each child is different and individual.

This has all the signs of a "U" Turn in the making, and it is very good news indeed.

[65] Bullshit Mr. Clarke – Some justice!
November 19th, 2010

I urge the Government not to lose its compassion nor its sense of justice. Yet that is what the Coalition Government is in danger of doing when it "saves" £350m a year in legal aid costs.

I flag up two dangers. One is that this 'saving' disturbs the delicate balance between the rights of the citizen and the State, to the advantage of the State and the disadvantage of children with special educational needs. The other is that it lowers standards when it is all the more important to promote excellence in the care of those children, to make money go further.

This saving ought to be seen to be totally wrong. Maybe the Tories can't see it that way, although they should. They always assert this country's traditional values. The Lib Dems should surely see it as a blow to the rights of the individual, in particular the rights of the individual against the State.

There is a myth put about by those who would have you believe it - the Secretary of State for Justice and Lord Chancellor for examples – that tribunals are informal and non-legalistic.

The fact is that decisions taken there, as in any Court, are taken on the basis of the law – statutes, statutory regulations and cases that interpret them, make precedent. The man or woman in the street cannot be expected to know the way around – although somewhat stupidly there is the legal maxim that you are presumed to know the law; never mind somewhat stupid, very stupid.

My sad experience is that those appointed by the State to judge or to decide or even to arbitrate cannot always be expected to explain the law to them, or argue it out on their behalf against the State. Maybe they should, but they don't see it as their remit. It's not the way the system works.

My partner for many years volunteered her services and her legal know-how in the Tribunal Unit of a Citizen's Advice Bureau before it was closed down by a local authority. She also served as a wing member of a Disability Tribunal. I saw it through her eyes and I also through my own. I saw it as a governor of special school witnessing the efforts of parents to get their children into a school a local authority wanted to close in pursuit of the policy of the day.

This is the reason why Legal Aid is a core value in a democratic Western Society. There should be a line in the sand beyond which these cuts should not go, and this "cut" is beyond that line.

Consider a case in the House of Lords. It ruled that teachers and those working for local education authorities, had a duty of care to children with Special needs. The Local Authorities tried to argue that as Parliament, in establishing the Statementing process to protect children, had not provided this – in fact it had actually rejected an amendment to this effect – it had limited the duty of care to the Statementing process, and that was the end of their responsibility.

Seven Lord Justices decided otherwise – thank Heavens.

They said quite specifically that whether Local Authorities liked it or not, whether teachers liked it or not, whether it produced a rash of claims or not, whether it was difficult to put a figure to the damages caused or not, teachers, education officers, educational psychologists, all those working for Local Authorities had a duty of care, and the Local Authorities had what is called a vicarious liability, that is an indirect but real liability, for any failure on the part of their employees to provide it. That failure is called negligence.

Local Authorities could not even argue that they had to address only the child's educational needs. The judges again were explicit. **"They have to take reasonable care of their health and safety including the monitoring of their needs and performance."**[8]

It is in this context that Kenneth Clarke, Secretary of State for Justice and Lord Chancellor, said this in Parliament.

"We believe it is simply not right for the taxpayer to help inject an element of what is really legalism into problems that should in the end be resolved taking into account the best interests of the child from an educational point of view."

This is bullshit, Mr. Clarke!

I quote from a letter to the Editor of *The Times* from Professor Michael King, School of Law, University of Reading.

"The Government's plan to remove legal aid from parents on low incomes who seek to challenge local authority decisions on their children's special educational needs is yet another example of the UK ignoring its international law obligations (under the UN Children's rights Convention) to make children's interests a primary consideration in any state action concerning children. Not only will these proposed cuts prevent parents from obtaining legal help in the preparation of their tribunal case, it will make it impossible for them to secure a report from an independent psychologist or speech and language therapist at present paid for under legal aid to counter the often one-sided reports produced by local educational departments. ... many parents ...will be forced to accept the cheaper, and often woefully inadequate, services that cash-strapped local authorities will seek to impose."

So, standards of excellence – forget them!

The Wonderful Gift of Music
January 5th, 2011

I want to share with you an amazing 2 hours watching The Music Instinct on Sky Arts. This documentary should be compulsory viewing for all those interested in education, health care and the social sciences, and priority viewing for everyone else. Anthony Storr illustrated in his book *Music and the Mind*[11] that it can have a special value for children with learning difficulties. I am indebted to my music teacher who played records to us with, as I recall it, fibre tipped needles. If music is introduced at school, it will last a lifetime. It has for me. With great music like great art you can touch eternity. These are moments that will last a lifetime.

Strangely the programme did not explore, as Emma Kirk the music teacher does in Death of a Nightingale, whether music that can be termed spiritual – from anywhere in the world – reaches part of the brain that other music does not. But it did explore the way that music acts as a trigger to emotion – happiness, sadness, terror, and provides a stimulus to the imagination. *It also echoed my thought that it had been around since the dawn of civilisation. Archaeologists have discovered an ivory flute going back 30,000 years.*

Neuro-scientists studying brain function with the latest MRI scanners now have evidence that music in early years can improve cognitive skills, make those suffering from Parkinson's Disease more mobile, help stroke victims talk again, steady the heart beat of patients in intensive care units, contribute to the care of Alzheimer patients and offer great benefit to children with special education needs.

I ask the question. When children with special needs are being taught in mainstream schools are they all being introduced to music?

Terry is my favourite character in Death of a Nightingale, as there is a subplot to the play in the music lesson.

Is there a God? More precisely is God "God of the Jews", "God of the Christians", "God of the Muslims", "God of the Sikhs", "God of the "Tibetan monks" ... or just "God"? Or, alternatively, is God simply a figment of a very fertile imagination, a concept made by man in the image of man to give meaning to birth and death?

In this argument Terry is a younger version of Richard Dawkins, but perhaps even more disrespectful of authority. He echoes his father and the millions of those who doubt God's existence altogether. He is a fictional character, but he is very real.

Terry does not believe in God. Very early on in the Play we know he is an awkward customer. He loses friends easily, but gains secret admirers.

He stays that way until the very end, even when he has been put on Ritalin. Whether he should have been is, of course, another issue.

In the music lessons in the Play I look at the nature or otherwise of God's existence through the prism of music. In sporting terms it is Emma Kirk, the

Music Teacher, versus Terry. She certainly feels it is that way. The battle between Emma Kirk and Terry is joined.

Yes, Terry is my favourite character. You will sense by now that I like those who cock a snook at authority. But I shall give the last word to Tracy. She very much reminds me of a pupil I knew when I was a Governor of a Special School. This was her contribution to the battle.

"My Nana used to say that God was as near to her as a new born babe and as far away as the furthest star."

And she says it to music.

[I say Amen to that.]

Inclusion is a Monumental Cock-Up
March 25th, 2011

Inclusion is still a political hot potato. Mary Warnock called it a disaster. The Green Paper promised for last Autumn, has just been published. The question is - whose fingers is the potato burning?

By coincidence, drowned out by the Budget, yesterday's BBC News put out a report by the Specialist Schools and Academies Trust, with some alarming statistics. *'Research shows the number of children with disabilities has risen from 700,000 in 2004 to 950,000 in 2009.'* The report also said *'one in five pupils in England is said to have some form of special needs.'* This equates to around 1.7 million children.

Those who truly have special needs are being lost among those categorised as having them. This has happened because schools have seized the opportunity to get extra money for children with special needs on offer to make inclusion acceptable to mainstream schools, this along with the 100,000 classrooms assistants recruited for the same purpose – all regardless of expense! And there is no follow-up to any of this in this week's *Times Educational Supplement.* The drowning process goes on.

What has happened?

In a debate in the House of Lords[2] on school milk in October 1976 – you can imagine how many noble Lords will have been present – in a 41 minute debate an amendment to require LEAs to educate children with mainstream schools that had earlier in the year been rejected by disability organisations and the NUT was nevertheless approved, and was subsequently passed into law.

Thus, Parliament gave a legal right to children with special needs to mainstream education. An army has been recruited to try to make it work, and in some cases it has. In many cases it has not. Children have been given rights without benefits; substandard teaching and care, exclusion in an inclusive environment - and bullying.

Yes, sometimes the education of children without special needs has benefited from the presence of children with special needs. However, their right to have an education appropriate to their needs has not always been fully respected because of the demands made on time and limited know how of teachers made responsible for children with special needs?

The post performance discussion last night concluded that the lucky ones today are those in the remaining special schools, schools like Oak Lodge in Finchley and Barbara Priesman School in Sunderland that I helped parents save from the cull.

Furthermore, what some may have hoped would save money has actually become extraordinarily expensive.

So, why the media silence? Simply because all three political parties support inclusion, and academia validated it. Parliament sanctioned it and the media gave it their blessing.

Just think: a Blind Man playing Cricket
May 20 2011

I mention him in *Death of a Nightingale*. His name is Fred Raffle. I shall explain why later.

I want to consider here the distinction between disability and deprivation. I ask you which should cause greater concern?

One of the most remarkable things about my involvement as Chair of Governors of a special school for physically disabled children over many years was to discover what a moving and inspirational experience it was. It is against that background that I pose that question.

What I found particularly moving was seeing children learning to accept and overcome the difficulties that their disabilities presented them with, and the ever so patient help they received from their dedicated and highly trained teachers, carers and therapists.

In Death of a Nightingale I take you into its classrooms. It is a work of fiction, but fact is just below the surface and, from time to time, cuts through it.

Fred Raffle visited my local Rotary Club with his dog Barney to share with us his enthusiasm for the game of cricket, an enthusiasm he gained at a School for the Blind where he and others found a way of playing it with a bag of peas for the ball and a suitcase for the wicket.

The story of Helen Keller is even more astounding.[18]

The moral of the story – you have to cater for deprivation as well as disability.

End the Stigma – Pronto! Vivace!
May 27th, 2011

To sell the idea of mainstream education to parents of children with special needs under the banner of inclusion, they (politicians, mandarins, academics, with the media believing them) had to 'do down' special schools. They had, in a word, to stigmatise them. They described special schools as 'segregation', not treating kids like 'normal' kids. I even heard them describe the school I was a governor of as a 'ghetto'. I know what a ghetto is, and ghetto it was not. They described 'segregation' as a denial of human rights. I have argued elsewhere that 'a right without a benefit is no great 'right'.

Yes, I am sure that there were some bad special schools, just as there are bad mainstream schools. I was fortunate enough to see with my own eyes a very, very good one.

There is the episode of the parent demanding mainstream education for his child from David Cameron; TV reports implying that governments get it wrong if they don't provide it on request.

Another illustration - an article in *The Times* on Tuesday May 24 reported a remarkable story about Lewis Hamilton's brother, Nicholas. He is himself *"on track for a racing career, despite cerebral palsy."* It was a great story and a great human achievement. In the press report, Dad is quoted as saying *"If you have disabled kids don't put them in a special school – put them in a normal one. If they can't cope then make other provisions but give them a chance."*

I wouldn't know what *"other provisions"* he has in mind – but don't send your child to a special school? What outrageous nonsense! What a gratuitous slight on all those wonderfully dedicated teachers and carers who work in special schools.

That is how the process of stigmatising works, and *The Times* is as gullible as anyone in publishing it.

[I must tell] Mr. Hamilton, [senior that] teachers tell me that they are finding parents saying that LEA's raised their hopes that their children could be educated in 'normal' schools only to find, when they arrived, that they are bullied, find it difficult to make friends and [they are] excluded in an inclusive environment, just handed over to classroom assistants. Meanwhile teachers themselves can't cope.

It is not as though Nicholas Hamilton himself didn't have to tough it out. He was bullied and in bold print Nicholas himself says *"People have no idea of the effort I've had to get here."*

Not all children with special needs have the same edge as the Hamiltons. Some are much more vulnerable. I have just read the latest truancy figures, still on the rise. I wonder how many of these children have been bullied in mainstream schools and that is why their parents don't force them to go to school? Statisticians never seem to pose this question and the media never ask them to.

Yes, trumpet the success of mainstream schools in educating children with special needs, ie the ones that survive and thrive. I know that there's some great work going on there. But don't project narrow, singular experience for everyone else in ignorance of their needs, in ignorance of the provision that can be made to meet those needs elsewhere, and don't stigmatise special schools in the process.

The good news is that the Government has at long last seen the light. The recent Green Paper issued by the Department for Education wants to *'end the bias towards inclusion'*.

In response to the letter in the *Guardian* on Saturday 12th March 2011 about the SEN Green Paper by an eminent group of professors, Minister Sarah Teather MP wrote a trenchant reply:

'I was very disappointed to read the misrepresentation of the Government's Green Paper on special educational needs and disabilities. (Letters p.41 Saturday 12th March) The suggestion that Government is trying to make children with complex needs 'earn' a place in a mainstream school is both offensive and inaccurate. At the heart of the Green Paper is the importance of parental choice. Parents know what type of education they want for their child and they should be allowed to decide if that is a mainstream or special school, academy or free school. At no point do we suggest that one form of schooling is better or preferable for children with additional or complex needs – this is about parental choice, not the ideologically driven idea that the state knows best.'

The academics Sarah Teather is referring to are the people who don't want parents to have that choice because they continue to assert that inclusion is *'a socially just and fair approach to schooling with benefits for all.'* By implication special schools are socially unjust and unfair.

They have not the slightest interest in trying to see and meet the differing needs of these children and respect the wishes of their parents. They see that as turning the clock back. Another smear! And they smear the Green Paper too, " *For many, these proposals signal their likely exclusion not only from mainstream education, but also from whatever 'big society' this government intends to create."*

For the past thirty years Academia has treasured anything and everything that confirmed its view but binned everything and anything that didn't. They had worked it out in the libraries of their minds not in the classrooms of the real world [thirty years ago] in the nineteen seventies, and they've got stuck in the same groove ever since.

Just how long will they be allowed to stigmatise special schools, teach their students the error of their ways, and require their students to repeat them to pass their exams? How long must we wait for them to eat their words or, if they can't move their brains out of idling mode, take early retirement?

The late Flo' Wilkinson, a retired teacher who lived to the age of 105, when asked by the Chief Rabbi the secret of her longevity, replied "*Never stop learning.*" I commend that advice to that twaddle of professors and others like them.

KIDS IN SPECIAL SCHOOLS NOW THE LUCKY ONES!
June 20th, 2011

£3.4 billion (and rising) - the amount now spent annually on non-teaching classroom assistants to help facilitate the Inclusion of children into mainstream schools - according to Durham University's research for the Sutton Trust published in this week's MailOnline.

This is on top of the money paid to mainstream schools for those they categorise as having special educational needs to help them cope – when many haven't special education needs at all.

The MailOnline on 20 June 2011 records:

"But perhaps more stark is the finding that hiring more classroom assistants has only a 'very small or no effect' on attainment. While they can have a 'positive effect' on pupils' attitudes to work, they negatively impact on standards when used as a replacement for teachers. The number of teaching assistants rocketed under Labour and their rise has continued under the Coalition government, with around 214,000 hired this year so far."

Note the word "negatively". The English just love their understatements.

A teaching assistant's salary varies from £16,000 to over £20,000, about double the entire cost of the education of a child in a special school – £3.4 billion cost overall, nearly a four fold increase since the closure of over 100 special schools

The Sutton Trust Teaching Guide says it all: *'Very low/no impact for high cost"* and sets out better ways to spend the "pupil premium" giving better value for money'.

Thousands of children with special needs are being off-loaded on to these 'amiable mums' instead of being in the hands of trained and dedicated teachers and carers in special schools. How on earth does the 'twaddle of professors' justify this?

When will they face the sad reality that their Alice in Cloud Cuckooland dream of inclusion is clearly neither fair nor just for many children – and too expensive! No wonder no-one wants to talk about it.

The kids in Special Schools are now the lucky ones!

NO CHEERS FOR ACADEMIA – Naught out of ten!
March 28th, 2011

Professor Ralph Wedgwood, professor of philosophy at Merton College Oxford, and Christine Taylor, its Development Officer, came to *Death of a Nightingale* at the New End Theatre, Hampstead last week.

Here is my email to them:

What made the whole thing more poignant for me was to meet up with a member of the Wedgwood family. You would see, more than most, the bulldozing of Brighouse School as a metaphor for the destruction of valued possessions and the erosion of excellence in our society. When I was living in Sunderland I saw the demise of another great company with even older provenance, Hartley Wood making stained glass for cathedrals, stained glass having come to the North East at the time of Adam Bede.

There has to be something very badly wrong with this country to allow the destruction of its manufacturing base, as against other European countries that have managed to protect theirs. The fine brains in Oxford really should have directed their thoughts to understand the reason.

For me I now go back, as I said, to the lectures by the eminent Herbert Hart, the one bit of academic learning I truly value from my Merton days. I sense that you can trace the problem to the words people use and the way they use them. They condition their thoughts; in today's world 'programme' them.

Hence in the 72 posts in my Blog, I look at words like Equality and Rights and see how they are used and abused, and I look the word Equity/fair play and seeing how it is undervalued. In particular I see the legal rights that don't carry benefits you can sometimes better be without, and Equality, so far from being fair as lawyers assert, sometimes monstrously unfair and unwise.

I argue at the outset of these posts, the UK needs a detox, and that this is where you should begin.

These are philosophical thoughts, surely, and I would welcome an opportunity to discuss them further with you.

There are constitutional thoughts as well. How Inclusion became Law, starting with an amendment to the Education Bill in 1976 in a debate on school milk in the House of Lords.[2] How the checks and balances that I always thought were in place to combat the abuse of power have, one by one, been disabled; Helena Kennedy's Power Inquiry[10] in 2004 disabled before it was even enabled!

The other thing I am sure that you will have picked up from your visit is my criticism of my own time at Oxford. While I enjoyed and benefited from the experience, in retrospect the subjects I covered in jurisprudence were a preparation for life as a legal 'termite', preserving an archaic system more interested in perpetuating itself than serving the interests of justice for the general public.

A study of other contemporary legal systems would have been much more useful than Roman Law and International Law. Apart from anything else – and there would have been much else – that would have shown me and others that you do not need to divide lawyers between the barristers and solicitors. This serves to keep the meter ticking longer, puts up the cost of justice and favours the powerful against the weak and state patronage.

I could have benefited from some pro bono work in tribunals where rules and regulations, law and precedent place unrepresented claimants at a huge disadvantage. I know this personally because my wife with her law degree represented claimants on behalf of Sunderland CAB until the Local Authority closed it down for the sake of a £50k saving.

Also, I would have benefited from some psychology in my studies. It was only later that I realised that the world was not the rational place that academics and lawyers behaved as though it were.

You will also have picked up the reference to professors criticising the 'individualised approach' to teaching. The line in the play that Tom Scott, its director, didn't like and edited out, is the comment that *" these professors go on to teach their students the error of their ways, and their students have to repeat them to pass their exams. UGH"* He preferred more simply *'And they go on to teach this nonsense to their students.'*

The full quote belongs to Professor Alan Dyson of Manchester University.

"We need, for many children at least, to abandon the individualised approach that has become the shibboleth of special needs education. Children with difficulties do not come into schools in ones – they come in 10s, scores, even hundreds. Instead of a case-by-case approach, we need robust organisational and teaching strategies, which schools can routinely use on whole groups of learners.

We should acknowledge that the difficulties experienced by many children arise not from their individual characteristics but from their social and family circumstances. The problems they face are compounded by structures of schooling, which marginalise their interests. Therefore, we should seek structural responses. Some of these must address broad social and economic issues. Some will have to look again at the underlying structures of the education system – such as competition between schools, and the impact of target-setting."

Of course, the worst-case scenario is where academics become the consultants to Government, feeding back what it wants to hear. I am pretty sure that Prof. Dyson was one of the people writing the report entitled *Costs and Outcomes for pupils with moderate learning difficulties in Special and Mainstream Schools 1999.*[4] *'It is important to be clear, therefore, that an analysis of costs and outcomes cannot properly be used to determine questions of rights.'* Do you endorse that?

This report, when you look at the detail, should have been referred back relying as it did on a 9% response from145 LEAs who 'sent information or undertaking studies'. It was the blind leading the blind. And no doubt Alan Dyson's students were themselves blindfolded, and had to go along with this way of thinking or fail their exams.

Prof. Dyson is just one of a cohort of academics subscribing to the dogma of Inclusion, treasuring anything that supports it, binning anything that doesn't – the archetypal termite – stigmatizing special schools in the process. They all delete my emails without reading them. Well, *Death of a Nightingale* is my response. I dare say they'd like to bin that too. In the closing words of Tracy, *"I'm not going to blow away in the wind."* Then if Brighouse School is a metaphor for all those good things destroyed by vandals, SEN is a metaphor for the West's whole approach to a lot of other things, almost everything that can be labelled a cock-up from Enron and the Credit Crunch right down to the closing of that CAB in Sunderland.

Alan

I am still awaiting that dialogue with my old college.

Jan Woolf was a special needs teacher in London for many years. She has also been an events producer, cultural activist and film censor. She is now a writer, holding the first Harold Pinter writer's residency at the Hackney Empire in 2010, where her play Porn Crackers was produced. Fugues on a Funny Bone - her collection of short stories (inspired by some of the children she used to teach) has just been published. www.muswell-press.co.uk

Notes & Quotes

1 An OFSTED Report on a Special School 2010

(Oak Lodge School, Finchley, provided actors for the stage production of Death of a Nightingale.)

"Oak Lodge is an outstanding school. The care, guidance and support which all staff provide are exemplary, ensuring that students gain excellent personal, social and learning skills. All students make outstanding progress in their academic learning regardless of ethnicity, gender or their special educational needs. This is based on extremely high-quality teaching and learning. There are rigorous and robust systems in place to set challenging targets and monitor students' progress. These are used extremely well by teachers in their planning. The school is beginning to use its data to make comparisons with similar schools, but as yet this underplays how well it is doing.

Safeguarding procedures are exemplary and students indicate that they feel safe and secure in Oak Lodge. Relationships between staff and students are excellent and are a crucial factor in the school's success. Students thoroughly enjoy school and say that lessons are fun. Attendance is good, even though a number of students have medical needs which require regular treatment. Behaviour is exemplary and staff manage challenging occurrences extremely well so that the learning of others is not disrupted. The curriculum is very carefully tailored to match students' needs, and the school quickly adapts its provision to meet the changing needs of its population. Through the focused development of their literacy, numeracy and information and communication technology skills (ICT) and their personal skills, students are extremely well prepared for the next stage of their education.

The school makes every effort to involve parents and carers actively in their children's learning. Staff are aware that sometimes the distance between home and school makes immediate communication a challenge, particularly in helping their children at home. Plans to use the school website in a more interactive way to address the concerns of a small minority of parents and carers are at an advanced stage.

The head teacher provides the vision, commitment and determination to lead the school forward. She is well supported by the senior leadership team and they have established very effective teamwork between the teachers and support staff. Staff development is given the highest priority and the input of staff is highly valued and acted upon so that all strive to improve the school even further. The school uses its specialist status very effectively so that partnerships with others are used extremely well to promote the learning and well-being of its own students and those in other local schools and colleges. The sixth form has developed extremely well since the last inspection and is now a strength of the provision. The governing body provides excellent challenge to the school and ensure that all statutory requirements are met. The commitment of all staff and governors to getting the best for students ensures that the school is extremely well placed to maintain its current strengths and improve in future."

[Is this school socially unjust and unfair? Visit Post 74 Death of a Nightingale Blog?]

2 An Exposé - the origins of Inclusion in the UK

Read Robin Jackson's review of **SPECIAL EDUCATIONAL NEEDS: A NEW LOOK** IMPACT: No. 11 in a series of policy discussions Mary Warnock

http://www.bjdd.org/new/pdf2006/Jan06_Book_Review_65-71.pdf

An extract

The fact is that in comparison with earlier government commissioned enquiries (e.g., Plowden, Newsom, Robbins) the Warnock Report achieved relatively little, partly because there were not the resources to fund significant changes and partly because the Warnock Committee had been forced to accept the case for integration which had already been set out in Section 10 of the 1976 Education Act.

Parliamentary process

On 1st July 1976, Clause 17 of the Education Bill was debated for the first time in the House of Commons. The aim of the clause was to change the emphasis of education for the handicapped from provision in special schools to provision in ordinary schools. From an examination of *Hansard* it is evident that there was persistent confusion among MPs as to the different meanings of the two central concepts – 'handicap' and 'integration'. Those speeches in favour of integration referred only to the predicament of the child and adult with a physical disability. However, for a number of reasons, Clause 17 never reached a third reading largely because there was some doubt about the costs of implementing a policy of integration. The debate in the House of Commons was uncontroversial with no party divisions. The only difference of opinion was between those advocating integration of pupils with physical disabilities into ordinary schools and those who sought to assess the practicality of the proposal. The assurance given by Miss Margaret Jackson, the Under-Secretary of State for Education and Science, that Clause 17 was not essential was the deciding factor. She doubted the necessity of a legal requirement to integrate, as it was her belief that integration could be successfully achieved without further legislation Clause 17 was withdrawn.

Given that ministerial assurance one might have thought that would have been the end of the story. But on 29th July 1976 the amended Education Bill, that had been passed in the Commons, reached the House of Lords.

In introducing the Bill, Lord Donaldson, Minister of State for Education and Science, spoke at length on those clauses in the Bill which related to the implementation of comprehensive secondary education. Discussion on these clauses lasted several months.

However on the 7th October, whilst the House was debating the subject of school milk, Baroness Phillips introduced Clause 10, which was a slightly altered but still recognisable version of Clause 17 which had been withdrawn three months earlier in the Commons.

Lord Donaldson pointed out that acceptance of this new clause would constitute an overnight reversal of policy of a kind for which there were neither the resources nor the goodwill on the part of many authorities to implement. One person who spoke strongly in favour of the new clause was Lord Vaizey who in doing so made reference to Mary Warnock who he stated was "a very old friend and colleague of mine from my days at Oxford". This remark may have been calculated to give the impression that he was in some way speaking on her behalf. He went on to speak of the length of time which committees such as the Warnock Committee generally took in reporting. He observed that this would be the last occasion for some time for Parliament to amend the law on this subject. This observation paid little regard to the constitutional niceties, disregarding, as it did, the fact that the Warnock Committee had been commissioned by the previous government to make recommendations on the issue of integration.

The debate was concluded by Baroness Phillips who argued that the inclusion of Clause 10 could not be construed as being 'revolutionary', as Lord Donaldson had claimed, and that it should be passed. And so it was!

What is revealing here is that the rational and balanced debate in the Commons was superseded by what *Hansard* showed to be an emotional, ill-informed and superficial discussion in the House of Lords. In that discussion there was no reference to any research data or indeed evidence of any kind, other than reference to individuals, most of whom were highly privileged, and with whom the speakers were personally acquainted.

It soon became evident that Section 10 (formerly Clause 10) had been introduced as a result of pressure applied by a small, powerful and readily identifiable lobby which represented the interests of a minority within the 'handicapped' population (i.e., physically handicapped/intellectually able). The tactics employed by this lobby succeeded in outmanoeuvring the government, the Department of Education and Science and most of the professional organisations. It was a pre-emptive strike taken by a lobby that had concluded that the Warnock Committee might not at the end of its deliberations give unqualified support for a policy of integration.

What is disturbing from a constitutional standpoint is the fact that a handful of privileged and non-elected members of the Upper House were able to introduce an important legislative change on the basis of an ill-informed debate which, according to *Hansard*, lasted less than 41 minutes. The change proposed was of a fundamental nature and one that ran counter not only to the expressed wishes of the government but to the views of most professional and voluntary organisations.

Critical reaction

The introduction of Section 10 caused an instant tidal wave of critical reaction. The National Association of Schoolteachers/Union of Women Teachers issued a statement on the 7th October which was published in

The Times citing difficulties in implementing the proposals. A letter from Mary Warnock was published in *The Times Educational Supplement* of the 11th November criticising the inclusion of Section 10.

A *Times* leader on the 11th November observed that the new legislation would lead to considerable controversy. On the 19th November *The Times* carried a letter from Mary Warnock repeating her concern that the clause had been passed precipitately. It is interesting to contrast the ways in which the inclusion of Clause 10 in the Education Bill was subsequently reported. One account of the debate is provided by the Association of Disabled Professionals – the organisation which had featured so prominently in the 'evidence' cited during both debates in Parliament. The introduction of the Clause was described as the logical denouement of rational debates in both Houses of Parliament. Satisfaction was expressed that there had been no real controversy in either debate!

The fact that the government spokesman in the House of Lords had urged that the amendment be withdrawn in order that Parliament could await the findings of the Government Committee of Enquiry was ignored.

The foreword to the National Union of Teacher's booklet *Special Education in Ordinary Schools* published in 1977 made it clear that the inclusion of this clause in the Bill was quite unexpected .... (NUT, 1977). Serious doubts were also expressed as to the effects of implementing Section 10. In the NUT's view this could not be seen as progress but rather a decline in the provision of special education, and a subsequent deterioration of educational opportunities for children with disabilities. Reference was also made to the fact that the NUT had submitted evidence to the Warnock Committee warning it against approving a policy of integration.

In arguing so strongly and passionately for the inclusion of Clause 10, one might have thought that Baroness Phillips and her fellow peers were representing a majority view. But a close examination of the evidence submitted to the Warnock Committee by a cross-section of twenty professional and voluntary organisations reveals quite a different picture (Hayhoe, 1981). Whilst most organisations sympathised with *the principle of integration*, the majority favoured it for groups of children *other than those they represented*. All were concerned that certain arrangements had to be put in place before integration could be successfully carried out. Those organisations which were most favourably disposed to integration were all concerned with educational provision for children with physical disabilities.

3 The Case for Inclusion - The Salamanca Statement

More than 300 participants representing 92 governments and 25 international organisations met in Salamanca, Spain in June 1994 to further the aim of *'Education for All'*. This was to consider what basic policy changes were needed to promote inclusive education so that *"schools could serve all children, particularly those with special educational needs."*

I hope that setting it out here will not switch you off. You need to read it to see the ideological content of the Inclusion policy. It is copied directly from http://www.inclusion.com on the Internet.

THE SALAMANCA STATEMENT: NETWORK for ACTION on SPECIAL NEEDS EDUCATION Adopted by the World Conference on Special Needs Education: Access and Quality Salamanca, Spain, 7-10 June 1994 Organised by the Government of Spain and UNESCO, the Conference adopted the Salamanca Statement on Principles, Policy and Practice in Special Needs Education and a Framework for Action. These two documents are important tools for efforts to make sure schools work better and to fulfil the principle of Education for All. They are printed in a single publication published by UNESCO. Get hold of a copy from the UNESCO office in your country or from the address at the bottom of this page. When you are familiar with its contents, use the two documents to lobby your government for improvements in the education of disabled children and for inclusive education policies.

The Salamanca Statement says that:

- every child has a basic right to education
- every child has unique characteristics, interests, abilities and learning needs
- education services should take into account these diverse characteristics and needs
- those with special educational needs must have access to regular schools

- regular schools with an inclusive ethos are the most effective way to combat discriminatory attitudes, create welcoming and inclusive communities and achieve education for all
- such schools provide effective education to the majority of children and improve efficiency with cost- effectiveness.

The **Salamanca Statement** asks governments to:

- give the highest priority to making education systems inclusive
- adopt the principle of inclusive education as a matter of law or policy
- develop demonstration projects
- encourage exchanges with countries which have experience of inclusion
- set up ways to plan, monitor and evaluate educational provision
- for children and adults
- encourage and make easy the participation of parents and organisations of disabled people
- invest in early identifi cation and intervention strategies
- invest in the vocational aspects of inclusive education
- make sure there are adequate teacher education programmes

Phil Wills MP, former Lib Dem spokesman for Education, said in the Commons on 20 March 2001: "Working in Chapeltown in the late 1960's convinced me that unless we could educate the whole community together - wherever they came from and whatever their needs and disabilities - frankly we would breed dysfunctional communities. It is a point of principle to me and my colleagues that inclusive education goes to the heart of the education system."

http://inclusion.uwe.ac.uk/csie provides comprehensive information.

4 Defective Academic Research

Extracts from *Costs and Outcomes for Pupils with Moderate Learning Difficulties in Special and Mainstream Schools 1999*

p 14 We have some generalized findings on outcomes from our literature survey and these are highly suggestive - but they do not make it possible to evaluate the cost-effectiveness of the schools in our study... For many, inclusion is a fundamental human right - not simply one form of SEN provision amongst many, to be evaluated on the balance of advantage it confers on children. *It is important to be clear, therefore, that an analysis of costs and outcomes cannot properly be used to determine questions of rights.*

(My italics – note one classroom assistant costs more than the entire cost of a pupil's education in a special school.)

P71 The state of our knowledge about outcomes for pupils with MLD is not good, and our understanding of the relationship between costs and outcomes is even worse.

P 107 Appendix 4 LEA Survey

Requests for information = 145 excluding 8 LEAs involved in the research
33 LEAs responded to this request:

- 76% do not have any information/studies
- 15% sent limited information but do not have any significant current studies.
- 9% sent information or undertaking studies.

Deliver us from social ills

Published in Times Educational Supplement 23 June, 2000 - Professor Alan Dyson co-director at the special needs research centre, department of education, University of Newcastle.

We have to move away from the idea of "Warnock's 18 per cent". This definition of who is vulnerable in our schools excludes groups which fail to make it nto the special needs category - groups such as children from cultural, ethnic and linguistic minorities, children who are disaffected from school and even some able and talented children. At the same time, it creates a tenuous alliance between quite disparate groups of children who share little other than the special needs label. It is surely time to abandon this one-size-fits-all approach.

We need, for many children at least, to abandon the individualised approach that has become the shibboleth of special needs education. Children with difficulties do not come into schools in ones - they come in 10s, scores, even hundreds. Instead of a case-by-case approach, we need robust organisational and teaching strategies which schools can routinely use on whole groups of learners.

We should acknowledge that the difficulties experienced by many children arise not from their individual characteristics but from their social and family circumstances. The problems they face are compounded by structures of schooling which marginalise their interests. Therefore, we should seek structural responses. Some of these must address broad social and economic issues. Some will have to look again at the underlying structures of the education system - such as competition between schools, and the impact of target-setting. Debates around these issues have effectively been silenced in recent years, but they are now urgently needed.

5 The dream turns sour!

Unpleasant experiences of parents of children with special needs in the UK today.

Visit http://news.bbc.co.uk/1/hi/education/7530895.stm

Who are the *"low achieving pupils"* in the UK.
Visit http://news.bbc.co.uk/1/hi/education/7543774.stm

The Bullying of Children with Learning Disabilities
- ENABLE Scotland 2007

Our work with our Young People's Self Advocacy Groups has revealed that bullying is also an important issue for children and young people with learning disabilities. We joined forces with Mencap to undertake UK wide research to find out the scale and nature of the problem and most importantly to tell us more about how to stop it.

We knew that bullying of children with learning disabilities existed. We knew that it is widespread and has a significant effect on children's lives.

However, we were shocked by the results that the survey revealed. We could not have predicted the scale of the problem.

- The sheer numbers of children who were bullied
- The persistence of bullying throughout childhood
- The failure of adults to stop bullying when it is reported
- The range of places where bullying takes place
- The effects bullying has on the emotional state of children The social exclusion faced by children who are afraid to go out

Bullying is not just a part of growing up. ENABLE Scotland believes that no child should have to put up with bullying and that we all have a responsibility to speak up to ensure that this stops.

Headline Results

- 93% of children with learning disabilities have been bullied
- 46% of children with learning disabilities have been physically assaulted
- Half have been bullied persistently for more than two years
- Bullying is not just a school issue
- 40% are too scared to go to places where they have been bullied
- **7 Extracts from Education Policy Partnership,**

December 2003 Review - *The impact of paid adult support on the participation and learning of pupils in mainstream schools*

A recent government consultation paper on the role of school support staff DfES, 2002 indicated that there were over 100,000 working in schools - an increase of over 50 percent since 1997.

- Paid adult support staff can sometimes be seen as stigmatising the pupils they support. Paid adult support staff can sometimes thwart inclusion by working in relative isolation with the pupils they are supporting and by not helping their pupils, other pupils in the class and the classroom teacher to interact with each other.
- Paid adult support shows no consistent or clear overall effect on class attainment scores. Paid adult support may have an impact on individual but not class test scores.

- Most significantly, there is evidence from several studies of a tension between paid adult support behaviour that contributes to short-term changes in pupils, and those which are associated with the longer-term developments of pupils as learners. Paid adult support strategies associated with on-task behaviour in the short term do not necessarily help pupils to construct their own identity as learners, and some studies in this cluster suggest that in such strategies can actively hinder this process.
- Paid adult support staff can positively affect on-task behaviour of students through their close proximity. Continuous close proximity of paid adult support can have unintended, negative effects on longer-term aspects of pupil participation and teacher engagement. Less engaged teachers can be associated with the isolation of both students with disabilities and their support staff, insular relationships between paid adult support staff and students, and stigmatisation of pupils who come to reject the close proximity of paid adult support.
- Given current interest in involving users in planning, carrying out and evaluating research, it is surprising that so few studies actually focus on the pupils' views.

6 Alarm bells ring

Enabling Inclusion: Blue Skies...Dark Clouds? (Professional excellence in schools) edited by Tim O'Brien 2001

Gary Hornby, Senior Lecturer in SEN, University of Hull:

In a recent review of the research on teacher perceptions of inclusion, *Scruggs and Mastropieri (*1996) analysed the results of twenty-eight studies published between 1958 and 1995. The major finding was that, although, on average 65 per cent of teachers supported the general concept of inclusion, only 40 per cent of teachers believed that this is a realist goal for most children...only 33 per cent of teachers believed that mainstream classroom was the best place for children with disabilities. Only 28 per cent of teachers thought that there was sufficient time to implement inclusion and only 29 per cent thought that they had sufficient expertise. ... *Croll and Moses* (2000) have recently found similar reservations among teachers in the UK.

Tim O'Brien

The trouble with a bandwagon is that it can all too easily become a run-a-way train.

Philip Garner, Professor in education, University of Northampton

Underlying this is my belief that to promote inclusion in an era of competition - at every level of education service - is an unforgivable deceit, in that it uses disadvantaged learners, and their teachers, as pawns in a Machiavellian drive to secure power through moral authority....Most crucially it impacts on the educational opportunities and life chances of those who have disabilities and learning difficulties.

.....If, as those most closely involved in inclusion-related teacher education, we say goodbye to the benign, pupil-orientated notion of Mr Chips, it is all bound to end in tears. Above all else we should not be side-tracked down a blind alley of debating fatuous, pious and ultimately discriminating terminologies — however benign they might sound. What are needed, on the ground are actions not words.

Charles Gains

Given all this, I conclude that current pressures to include are externally driven and based largely on political and ideological demands rather than cool and informed consideration. In my opinion, this *melange* invites disaster.

BBC News 16 December 2009

The National Autistic Society's chief executive, Mark Lever, said: *"A great many parents of children and young people with autism have to fight huge battles to get the education support that should be theirs by right, often at considerable emotional and financial expense.*

"We hear terrible stories from parents of local authorities flouting the law by ignoring diagnoses, not meeting statutory timescales, failing to write statements properly, and even saying they 'don't do' statements any more.

"It is hardly surprising then that parents have little confidence in the special educational needs system, and they could be forgiven for thinking that this report will do little to change what for them is an often complicated, intimidating, and sometimes infuriating system."

MailOnline Monday June 20 2011

Research by the Sutton Trust found that, when it comes to spending the Pupil Premium, almost three-quarters (73 per cent) of teachers see cutting class sizes as one of their top three priorities.

But perhaps more stark is the finding that hiring more classroom assistants has only a 'very small or no effect' on attainment.

While they can have 'positive effect' on pupils' attitudes to work, they negatively impact on standards when used as a replacement for teachers.

The number of teaching assistants rocketed under Labour and their rise has continued under the Coalition government, with around 214,000 hired this year so far.

The Independent, 14 July 2011

Dr. Martin Stephen just retired as High Master of St Paul's School in west London "Lessons from the Future"

"We will stop interpreting the basic human right of equal opportunity as mean that all children must only have the same opportunity."

The Times Educational Supplement, 5 August 2011

What keeps me awake at night - I trained to teach, not nurse

Anonymous views from education's front line
This week: a primary teacher in Yorkshire

I didn't do that well at school. When I say I didn't do too well, what I mean is that I achieved five GCSE grades at C or above. I passed all the others too, but they consisted of a few Ds, Es ... you know how it goes. I shuffled into a place at sixth-form and managed to scrape one pass out of the experience.

My excuse is that I simply wasn't ready to learn. Some people aren't - it took me until my mid-20s to realise I was ready to work at somewhere near the academic level I knew I was capable of.

After flirting with the idea of an access course in nursing (but eventually enrolling on the education course) and achieving a degree in education with honours and qualified teacher status, I began to teach. The whole process of becoming a teacher took me five years. A long time, don't you think?

Bearing this in mind, I was somewhat surprised to find in my first year that I would be taking on the role of a nurse by administering drugs to a diabetic three times a day - and as and when they were needed - having had no medical training.

I had a meeting with the child's nurse, headteacher, my teaching assistant and parents. It lasted over an hour and was a training session on how to use the child's intravenous insulin, his Bluetooth widget and cannula injection thingy.

I couldn't get my head around the units of insulin required, what to do if the child was hypo, hyper, or just plain hyperactive. I didn't understand what the various pieces of equipment really did, or how to read them in the first place. I struggled with the huge responsibility - and it is huge - of administering the insulin and simply getting it right. The risks involved were colossal: get it wrong and the child could enter some kind of diabetic coma or worse. That never happened, but then again that's not the point.

I had to count the child's calories, measure what he ate and when (which involved sitting with him while he ate lunch to ensure he didn't have something he shouldn't have had) and then enter the information correctly into the Bluetooth thingy.

I can't repeat it enough, but all this without a sniff of a first-aid certificate. I may sound like a whiner to many of you, moaning about my responsibilities as a teacher. But this is the problem: I'm a teacher, not a nurse. I didn't want to administer drugs to a child, and I certainly didn't want that level of responsibility in my NQT year. I'm not convinced I would like it now. Not ever, in fact.

What can one do, though? Is it fair to become a conscientious objector in your own classroom when dealing with the needs of the children you're there to teach? Maybe I should have considered the access course to nursing after all.

The Sunday Times 14 August 2011 Answer the question

For the last two years our nine-year old son has been in a class at his school with a child who has Asperger's syndrome. This child often hits and kicks other children and the situation seems to be tolerated more than it would be for a child without special needs. Our son has been hit and kicked and even, on one occasion, strangled. ...

Name withheld

7 A change of policy

Extracts from House of Commons Education and Skills Committee - Third Report March *2007 A confused message*

65. It is widely presumed that the Government has a policy of inclusion or an inclusion agenda. Indeed, Baroness Warnock in her recent article—which many described as a u-turn in her position on inclusion —concluded that "possibly the most disastrous legacy of the 1978 report, was the concept of inclusion." She argued in the article that inclusion could be taken "too far" and that this was resulting in the closure of special schools to the detriment of children with SEN.

66. The Government has, in written and oral evidence to this Committee, repeatedly stated that "it is not Government policy to close special schools" and that "Government plays no role in relation to local authority [...] decisions to close schools."

77. The most radical u-turn was demonstrated by Lord Adonis in his evidence to the Committee. The Minister described the Government as being "content" if, as a result of Local Authority decisions, the current "roughly static position in respect of special schools" continues.

78. Lord Adonis specifically said that the Government: "do not have a view about a set proportion of pupils who should be in special schools."

79. This directly contradicts the stated aim in the 2004 SEN Strategy that "the proportion of children educated in special schools should fall over time". The Minister's words demonstrate a significant change inpolicy direction.

5 July 2007 Schools Minister Andrew Adonis has announced a further £23 million to expand the number of SEN specialist schools over the next three years. This will mean around 150 schools becoming specialist SEN schools.

2010 Department for Education *Green Paper* "Support and aspiration: A new approach to special educational needs and disability" Consultation

To transfer power to professionals on the front line and to local communities we will: strip away unnecessary bureaucracy so that professionals can innovate and use their judgement; establish a clearer system so that professionals from different services and the voluntary and community sector can work together; and give parents and communities much more influence over local services.

We propose to:

- **give parents a real choice of school**, either a mainstream or special school. We will remove the bias towards inclusion and propose to strengthen parental choice by improving the range and diversity of schools from which parents can choose, making sure they are aware of the options available to them and by changing statutory guidance for local authorities. Parents of children with statements of SEN will be able to express a preference for any state-funded school – including special schools, Academies and Free Schools – and have their preference met unless it would not meet the needs of the child, be incompatible with the efficient education of other children, or be an inefficient use of resources. We will also prevent the unnecessary closure of special schools by giving parents and community groups the power to take them. *(My underlining)*

8 Rights

"Human Rights" - Extract from Essay 8 - Essays in Jurisprudence and Philosophy by H.L.A. Hart

Page 196 There is however no doubt that the conception of basic human rights has deeply affected the style of diplomacy, the morality, and the political ideology of our time, even though thousands of innocent persons still imprisoned or oppressed have not yet felt its benefits. The doctrine of human rights has at least temporarily replaced the doctrine of maximizing utilitarianism as the prime philosophical inspiration of political and social reform. It remains to be seen whether it will have such success as utilitarianism once had in changing the practices of governments for human good.

Special Needs - Legal Rights in UK

Clause 1 3, 2001 SEN Act: *'If a statement is maintained under section 324 for the child, he must be educated in a mainstream school unless that is incompatible with - a the wishes of his parent, or b the provision of efficient education for other children.'* My underlining

Catchpole v Buckingham County Council and another, The *Times* Law Reports on 18 March 1999, Lord Justice Thorpe said *"the local education authority had a duty to ensure that a child with special education needs was placed at a school that was appropriate. It was not enough for the school to be merely adequate."*

Phelps v Hillingdon Borough Council, Anderton v Clwyd County Council, Gower v Bromley London Borough Council and Jarvis v Hampshire Country Council. Times Law Reports, July 28, 2000. The House of Lords ruled that LEAs duty of care required them to *"have to take reasonable care of their health and safety including the monitoring of their needs and performance."*

9 Pupil perceptions

Moderate Learning Difficulties and the Future of Inclusion, Braham Norwich and Narcie Kelly, page 163.

Mainstream pupils, few of whom had special school experiences, had mostly positive views about special schools. Mainly negative views were held by about one in five, with slightly more, about a quarter, holding mixed views This was different for special school pupils, where the majority had had mainstream school experiences. For them, only about one in six had mainly positive views of mainstream schools, whereas about half had mixed views, with about a third having mainly negative views. This difference could be due to special school pupils' 'bad' experiences in the mainstream, and mainstream pupils' lack of experience of special schools.

10 The System

The Power Inquiry

This Inquiry was set up by the Joseph Rowntree Trust in 2004 to mark its centenary.

It established a Commission under the chair of Baroness Helena Kennedy QC, to investigate why the decline in popular participation and involvement in formal politics has occurred, to provide concrete and innovative proposals to reverse the trend and to explore how public participation and involvement can be increased and deepened. Its work was based on the primary belief that a healthy democracy requires the active participation of its citizens. It is completely independent of any political party or organisation. It works across the political spectrum and, most importantly, with people who feel that the political parties do not represent them anymore.

The Commission published its final report, *Power to the People*, in February 2006. The report outlined 30 recommendations for change, but most importantly it argues that there is a need for a re-balancing of power between the Executive and Parliament, between Central and Local Government and between the Citizen and the State. www.makeitanissue.org.uk.

From *Leadership* by Rudolph Giuliani

The New York City school system was never really going to improve until its purpose, its core mission, was made clear. What the system *should* have been about was educating its million children as well as possible. Instead, it existed to provide jobs for the people who worked in it, and to preserve those jobs regardless of performance. That's not to say that there weren't committed professionals at every level within the system. There were, and that's the shame of it. Those with their hearts in the right place were the ones who suffered most.

Until I could get everyone involved to sit together and agree that the system existed to educate children, fixing little bits of it was symbolic at best. Band-Aid solutions can do more harm than good. The system needed a new philosophy. It needed to say we're not a job protection system but a system at its core about children's enrichment. All rewards and risks must flow from the performance of the children. If you took a broken system and repaired just enough so that it could limp along, you lessened the chance that a real and lasting s lution could be reached.

That's why I resist partial control over a project. The schools should be made into a mayoral agency—like the Administration for Children's Services or the Fire Department— so the city can enact real solutions.

11 God - A Universal Creator

The Prophets

And what does God require of you. But to do justice, to love mercy and towalk humbly with your God. **Micah 6:8.** *And now abideth faith, hope, charity, these three; but the greatest of these is charity.* **1 Corinthians 13:13.** *Those who make a display of piety but have not committed their whole lives to compassionate action are like those who perform daily prayers as habit or as convention, without true awe, humility, and longing. Since their religion remainsmere pretence, the vessel of their being has not been fi lled with active kindness by the Source of Love.* **Koran 107:1-7**

The Alexandria Declaration *January 2002*

"In the name of God who is Almighty, Merciful and Compassionate, we, who have gathered as religious leaders from the Muslim, Christian and Jewish communities, pray for true peace in Jerusalem and the Holy Land, and declare our commitment to ending the violence and bloodshed that denies the right of life and dignity.

According to our faith traditions, killing innocent in the name of God is a desecration of His Holy Name, and defames religion in the world. The violence in the Holy Land is an evil which must be opposed by all people of good faith. We seek to live together as neighbours respecting the integrity of each other's historical and religious inheritance. We call upon all to oppose incitement, hatred and misrepresentation of the other.

Delegates:

- His Grace the Archbishop of Canterbury, Dr. George Carey
- His Eminence Sheikh Mohamed Sayed Tantawi, Cairo, Egypt
- Sephardi Chief Rabbi Bakshi-Doron
- Deputy Foreign Minister of Israel, Rabbi Michael Melchior
- Rabbi of Tekoa, Rabbi Menachem Froman International Director of Interreligious Affairs, American Jewish Committee, Rabbi David Rosen
- Rabbi of Savyon, Rabbi David Brodman
- Rabbi of Maalot Dafna, Rabbi Yitzak Ralbag
- Chief Justice of the Sharia Courts, Sheikh Taisir Tamimi
- Minister of State for the PA, Sheikh Tal El Sider
- Mufti of the Armed Forces, Sheikh Abdelsalam Abu Schkedem
- Mufti of Bethlehm, Sheikh Mohammed Taweel
- Representative of the Greek Patriarch, Archibishop Aristichos
- Latin Patriarch, His Beatitude Michel Sabbah
- Melkite Archbishop, Archbishop Boutrous Mu'alem
- Representative of the Armenian Patriarch, ArchbishopChinchinian
- Bishop of Jerusalem, The Rt. Rev. Riah Abu El Assal

The Dignity of Difference by Chief Rabbi, Lord Sacks

Page 55 (2nd edition) "So too in the case of religion. The radical transcendence of God in the Hebrew Bible means that the Infinite lies beyond our finite understanding. God communicates in human language, but there are dimensions of the divine that must forever elude us.

As Jews we believe that God has made a covenant with a singular people, but that does not exclude the possibility of other peoples, cultures and faiths finding their own relationship with God within the shared frame of the Noahide laws. These laws constitute, as **it** were, the depth grammar of the human experience of the divine: of what it is to see the world as God's work and humanity as God's image.

God is God of all humanity, but between Babel and the end of days no single faith is the faith of all humanity. Such a narrative would lead us to respect the search for God in people of other faiths and reconcile the particularity of cultures with the universality of the human condition."

The Great Partnership God, Science and the search for Meaning by Jonathan Sacks

Published by Hodder & Stoughton 2011

God loves diversity, not uniformity. That is a fact of theological as well as ecological significance. Every attempt to impose uniformity on diversity is, in some sense, a betrayal of God's purposes. One definition of fundamentalism, and an explanation of why it is religiously wrong, is that it is the attempt to impose a single truth on a diverse world.

(The God of Love)

If we believe in the God of Abraham, we know we cannot fully know God. We can merely see the effects of his acts. And that surely is true of the children of Abraham. We can see how, given their beliefs, people behave.

If they love and forgive, if they are open to others, if they respect their opponents as well as honouring their fellow believers, if they work for a better world by becoming guardians of the heritages of nature and culture, if they care about the future our grandchildren will inherit but we will not live to see, then they will be beloved of their fellow humans, and they will become true ambassadors of the God who loves those who perform acts of love.

The Seven Laws of Noah

Often referred to as the **Noahide Laws,** these are a list of seven moral imperatives which were given by God to Noah as a binding set of laws for all mankind. They have been recognised in the United States Congress: "Whereas Congress recognizes the historical tradition of ethical values and principles which are the basis of civilized society and upon which our great Nation was founded; whereas these ethical values and principles have been the bedrock of society from the dawn of civilization."

Sikhism,

This, the youngest of the world religions, is barely five hundred years old. Its founder, Guru Nanak, was born in 1469. Guru Nanak spread a simple message of "Ek Ong Kar": we are all one, created by the One Creator of all Creation. This was at a time when India was being torn apart by castes, sectarianism, religious factions, and fanaticism. He aligned with no religion, and respected all religions. He expressed the reality that there is one God and many paths, and the Name of God is Truth, "Sat Nam".

The foundation of Sikhism was laid down by Guru Nanak. Guru Nanak infused his own consciousness into a disciple, who then became Guru, subsequently passing the light on to the next, and so on. The word "Guru" is derived from the root words "Gu", which means darkness or ignorance, and "Ru", which means light or knowledge The Guru is the experience of Truth God.

Each one of the ten Gurus represents a divine attribute:

Guru Nanak - Humility
Guru Angad - Obedience
Guru Amar Das — Equality
Guru Ram Das - Service
Guru Arjan - Self-Sacrifice
Guru Hargobind - Justice
Guru Har Rai - Mercy
Guru Harkrishan - Purity
Guru Tegh Bahadur - Tranquillity
Guru Gobind Singh - Royal Courage
This is taken directly from www.sikhnet.com

His Holiness the 14th Dalai Lama, Tenzin Gyatso

His Holiness the 14th Dalai Lama, Tenzin Gyatso, is both the head of state and the spiritual leader of Tibet. He was born on 6 July 1935, to a farming family, in a small hamlet located in Taktser, Amdo, northeastern Tibet. At the age of two the child, who was named Lhamo Dhondup at that time was recognized as the reincarnation of the 13th Dalai Lama, Thubten Gyatso. The Dalai Lamas are believed to be manifestations of Avalokiteshvara or Chenrezig, the Bodhisattva of Compassion and patron saint of Tibet. Bodhisattvas are enlightened beings who have postponed their own nirvana and chosen to take rebirth in order to serve humanity.

Three Main Commitments in Life

Firstly, on the level of a human being, His Holiness' first commitment is the promotion of human values such as compassion, forgiveness, tolerance, contentment and self-discipline. All human beings are the same. We all want happiness and do not want suffering. Even people who do not believe in religion recognize the importance of these human values in making their life happier. His Holiness refers to these human values as secular ethics. He remains committed to talk about the importance of these human values and share them with everyone he meets.

Secondly, on the level of a religious practitioner, His Holiness' second commitment is the promotion of religious harmony and understanding among the world's major religious traditions. Despite philosophical differences, all major world religions have the same potential to create good human beings. It is therefore important for all religious traditions to respect one another and recognize the value of each other's respective traditions. As far as one truth, one religion is concerned, this is relevant on an individual level. However, for the community at large, several truths, several religions are necessary.

Thirdly, His Holiness is a Tibetan and carries the name of the 'Dalai Lama'. Tibetans place their trust in him. Therefore, his third commitment is to the Tibetan issue. His Holiness has a responsibility to act as the free spokesperson of the Tibetans in their struggle for justice. As far as this third commitment is concerned, it will cease to exist once a mutually beneficial solution is reached between the Tibetans and Chinese. However, His Holiness will carry on with the first two commitments till his last breath.
*www.**dalailama**.com*

The Three Faiths Forum

The Three Faiths Forum has worked to encourage harmony and confront prejudice for the last 14 years. Our objectives are to build lasting relationships between people of different faiths (and those of non-religious beliefs), to achieve a society where religious and cultural differences can co-exist through empathy, respect and engagement; and to encourage friendship, goodwill and understanding, especially between Muslims, Christians and Jews.

We are a non-religious organisation working with government, religious leaders, educators, students and other interfaith groups. The organisation was founded in 1997 by Sir Sigmund Sternberg, the late Shaikh Dr Zaki Badawi and Revd Dr Marcus Braybrooke, and was originally a forum where religious and community leaders could meet. Today we are an agent of change, actively promoting intercultural understanding and cooperation. We work in schools, universities and wider society, giving people the knowledge and skills to challenge stereotypes and misconceptions, communicate effectively and build new relationships with people from all cultural and religious backgrounds.

Promoting good inter faith relations

The Inter Faith Network for the UK was founded in 1987 to promote good relations between people of different faiths in this country. Its member organisations include representative bodies from the Baha'i; Buddhist; Christian; Hindu; Jain; Jewish; Muslim; Sikh; and Zoroastrian communities; national and local inter faith bodies; and academic institutions and educational bodies concerned with inter faith issues.

Understanding with integrity

The Network works with its member bodies to help make the UK a place marked by mutual understanding and respect between religions where all can practise their faith with integrity.

The Network's way of working is firmly based on the principle that dialogue and cooperation can only prosper if they are rooted in respectful relationships which do not blur or undermine the distinctiveness of different religious traditions.

The uncertainties of science

"I have never known in quite a long life to be faced with so many unanswered questions. It is quite extraordinary that young people speak and teach about the evolution of the Universe and the Big Bang, and yet we have no idea what 95 per cent of the matter and energy in the Universe consists of." Sir Bernard Lovell, *The Times* 2 June 2007.

Paul Robeson and Peekskill 4 September 1949

Why did a concert given by Paul Robeson in New York State provoke a riot? He was a singer with a fine bass voice, and the first to bring spirituals to the concert hall. He was a notable actor on stage and in film. But he was much else besides. His father had been a run-a-way slave later becoming a church minister. His mother came from an abolitionist Quaker family. He had won an academic scholarship to Rutgers University, the only black student on campus at the time, and one of three classmates accepted into Phi Beta Kappa. He was a noted sportsman and athlete.

It was, however, as a civil rights activist campaigning against lynching, and as a supporter of the Soviet Union after World War II, that provoked the savage backlash in Peekskill that Labor weekend in 1949. Over fifteen thousand people had attended the concert, and hundreds of them were injured, some seriously, as they tried to make their way home. He was an iconic figure in the fight against racial prejudice. In the Soviet Union he said that he found a country free of racial prejudice, and as he sang in concerts around the world he said that Afro-American spiritual music resonated to Russian folk traditions, and he preached their common humanity. Not everyone agreed with him at the time.

12 Music and the Mind

By Antony Storr

Music is the most mysterious and intangible of all forms of art, yet it is a deeply significant experience for a greater number of people than ever before. In this challenging book, a practicing psychiatrist examines music as a life-enhancing experience and discusses why it stimulates the mind, captivates the heart, and nurtures the soul, and how it restores our sense of personal wholeness. Drawing on great thinkers and composers, Storr explores the inner world of music, revealing its origins, contemplating its powers, and considering its contributions to human existence.

Anthony Storr writes: *"David, a six-year-old autistic boy, suffered from chronic anxiety and poor visual-motor co-ordination. For nine months, efforts had been made to teach him to tie his shoe laces to no avail. However, it was discovered that his audio motor co-ordination was excellent. He could beat quite complex rhythms on a drum, and was clearly musically gifted. When a student therapist put the process of tying his shoe-laces into a song, David succeeded at the second attempt."*

13 Equality

William Armstrong, living in 19 Century was the first engineer, inventor, scientist, to be made a peer. He built the first house lit by hydro-electricity, Cragside in Northumberland, his firm manufactured the machinery that lifted Tower Bridge, the guns and ships of war that helped defend this country, and much else besides. He was Newcastle's great benefactor in so many ways, not least in education and training. This is what his biographer Henrietta Heald writes in his biography entitled "William Armstrong, Magician of the North":

"He opposed the manipulation and regulation of labour in the quest for a more equal society, believing that individual ambition should be given a free rein within the law. 'Struggle for superiority is the mainspring for progress. It is an instinct deeply rooted in our nature. ... To what a dead level of mediocrity would our country sink if struggle for superiority were stamped out amongst us, and how completely would we fall back in the race of nations.'".

Perhaps that is why he has been airbrushed out of the fame to which he should most certainly be entitled, a man who lived in the real world not just in the world he wanted it to be.

Or perhaps it was because he was a "boss", an engineer, an armaments manufacturer, and he came from the North!

14 Pills

Pills and pills! Perpetual sunshine
Mental Health Supplement, in the *Times* 27 November 2007
"Between 1991 and 2001 antidepressant prescriptions in the UK rose from 9 million to 24 million a year." And they are still rising.

Ritalin of no long-term benefit, study finds

Guardian Unlimited 12 November 2007

Research released today raises questions about the long-term effectiveness of drugs used to treat attention deficit hyperactivity disorder (ADHD).

A team of American scientists conducting the Multimodal Treatment Study of Children with ADHD (MTA) has found that while drugs such as Ritalin and Concerta can work well in the short term, over a three-year period they brought about no demonstrable improvement in children's behaviour. They also found the drugs could stunt growth.

The research, which will be broadcast on the BBC Panorama programme tonight, shows that GPs in the UK prescribed ADHD drugs such as Ritalin and Concerta to around 55,000 children last year – at a cost of £28m to the NHS.

The MTA's warning about ADHD drugs constitutes something of a revised opinion. The scientists, who have been monitoring the treatment of 600 children across the US since the 1990s, concluded in 1999 that, after one year, medication worked better than behavioural therapy for ADHD. This finding influenced medical practice on both sides of theAtlantic and prescription rates in the UK have since tripled.

The report's co-author, Professor William Pelham, of the University of Buffalo, said: "I think we exaggerated the beneficial impact of medication in the first study. We had thought that children medicated longer would have better outcomes. That didn't happen to be the case. "The children had a substantial decrease in their rate of growth, so they weren't growing as much as other kids in terms of both their height and their weight. And the second was that there were no beneficial effects - none.

"In the short run [medication] will help the child behave better, in the long run it won't. And that information should be made very clear to parents." Dr Tim Kendall, of the Royal College of Psychiatrists, who is helping prepare new NHS guidelines for the treatment of ADHD, said: "A generous understanding would be to say that doctors have reached the point where they don't know what else to offer. "I hope we will be able to make recommendations that will give people a comprehensive approach to treatment and that will advise about what teachers might be able to do within the classroom when they're trying to deal with kids who have diffi cult problems of this kind. "I think the important thing is we have a comprehensive approach that doesn't focus on just one type of treatment." The new treatment guidelines will be published next year.

15 The Dome

This was originally built in London for the Millennium celebrations. It is the largest structure of its kind in the world. The circumference of The Dome exceeds 1km, and the fl oor-space is large enough to park 18,000 London buses! The Jubilee Line on the London Underground was extended to reach it. Financially it was a huge cost to the taxpayer, and as the Dome it was a very large white elephant *we* will never forget. It has, however, come right in the end. It is now O2, a spectacular entertainment complex. Once it was a showpiece for New Labour's vision of the UK, now it is a showpiece for capitalism, but at the taxpayers' expense. Mercifully it is not a Casino.

16 School Organisation Committees

These committees are independent statutory bodies set up under the provisions of the School Standards and Framework Act 1998. Their principal role is to examine proposals for the closure and/or opening of schools as brought forward by a Local Education Authorities. They comprise: representatives from the Local Authority, elected Councillor Members, and nominees from the Church of England, the Catholic Church, the Learning and Skills Council and from the School Group School Governor representatives from the Primary/Secondary and Special sector schools.

17 The Luddites

They were a social movement of English textile artisans in the early nineteenth century who protested — often by destroying textile machines— against the changes produced by the Industrial Revolution, which they felt threatened their livelihood.

18 Helen Keller

Helen Keller was born in Tuscumbia, Alabama, on June 27, 1880, to parents Captain Arthur H. Keller, a former officer of the Confederate Army, and Kate Adams Keller, cousin of Robert E. Lee. She was not born blind and deaf; it was not until nineteen months of age that she came down with an illness that did not last for a particularly long time, but it left her deaf and blind. At that time her only communication partner was Martha Washington, the 6-year old daughter of the family cook, who was able to create a sign language with Helen, so that by age seven, she had over sixty different signs to communicate with her family

In 1886, her mother Kate Keller was inspired by an account in Charles Dickens' *American Notes* of the successful education of another deaf blind child, Laura Bridgman, and travelled to a doctor in Baltimore for advice. He put her in touch with local expert Alexander Graham Bell, who was working with deaf children at the time. Bell advised the couple to contact the Perkins Institute for the Blind, the school where Bridgman had been educated, which was then located in South Boston, Boston, Massachusetts. The school delegated teacher and former student, Anne Sullivan, herself visually impaired and then only 20 years old, to become Keller's teacher. It was the beginning of 49-year-long relationship.

Helen's big breakthrough in communication came one day when she realized that the motions her teacher was making on her palm, while running cool water over her palm from a pump, symbolized the idea of "water;" she then nearly exhausted Sullivan demanding the names of all the other familiar objects in her world including her prized doll. Anne was able to teach Helen to speak using the Tadoma method touching the lips and throat of others as they speak combined with "fingerspelling" alphabetical characters on the palm of Helen's hand. Later, Keller would also learn to read English, French, German, Greek, and Latin in Braille.

In 1888, Keller attended the Perkins School for the Blind. In 1894, Keller and Sullivan moved to New York City to attend the Wright-Humason School for the Deaf and Horace Mann School for the Deaf. In1896 they returned to Massachusetts and Helen entered The Cambridge School for Young Ladies before gaining admittance, in 1900, to Radcliffe College, where Standard Oil magnate Henry Huttleton Rogers paid for her education. In 1904 at the age of 24, Keller graduated from Radcliffe magna cum laude, becoming the first deaf and blind person to graduate from a college.

Helen Keller wrote *Light in my Darkness*, which was published in 1960. In the book, she advocates the teachings of the Swedish scientist and philosopher Emanuel Swedenborg. She also wrote an autobiography called *The Story of My Life*, which was published in 1903.. In total, she wrote twelve books and authored numerous articles.
Extracted from Wikipedia

Questions for Quiet Contemplation

The play is about special education needs.

It also affords a peep-hole to a larger picture. In some ways it is a parable for our times. I am uncomfortable with the dogma of Inclusion. I also sense unease about the future of our world as we live off it, and you may feel it too. All things, after all, have their life cycle.

I worry that the words we use, words like Equality, Rights, and Inclusion actually imprison our thoughts, because we use them without thinking about them in the real world, not just the desirable one.

So I have allowed my mind to meditate on these things, and you may care to do the same.

There can always be renewal and refreshment.

People have asked me who I have written this for. The answer obviously is for anyone interested enough to want to read it. But I have had in my mind those who have a care and concern for the rising generation of children, in particular their parents, their teachers and those with specific responsibility for them. I pose questions especially for them - but not just for them - which they might like to think about.

I give some short answers knowing full well that there are sometimes very long answers or no easy answers at all. What I do know, however, is the power of the written and the spoken word. Way back in time it was transmitted from memory, more recently on the printed page, and now on the Internet. It is our greatest resource, and we must all use it.

Here are some questions I invite you to think about.

1. What stands between us and the destruction of things we treasure?
2. Who threatens it?
3. Where does our strength reside?

4. Which is the wiser mantra in education - Equality or Equity?
5. How far does declaring a "Right" provide the protection of "a Right"?
6. How do we reconcile an increasingly controlling society with a participating one?
7. How do we get a more efficient, less wasteful system of Government?
8. How do we get better directed policies from all political parties?
9. How does a multicultural society live at peace with itself?
10. Is this generation properly mindful of the legacy it is bequeathing to the grandchildren of its grandchildren?

My short answers

1. *A sense of our common humanity and an appreciation of our diverse needs*
2. *The common denominator here - all those who abuse their power over people. The little Hitlers as well as the big Hitlers, and not just politicians; people in all walks of life, religious as well as secular.*
3. *In life force and in the human spirit. So encourage the young to aspire, to work together, to put a value on self-esteem and to uphold standards of conduct and behaviour.*
4. *One child's opportunity can be another child's road block. What is important is that the children are equal or unequal, but that they are all different. I go for Equity every time.*
5. *Sometimes, but certainly not always. A right without a benefit is more than useless.*
6. *Structure in that participation ... and make it stick. Lip service is not enough. Those who say that they want to achieve this should say how they plan to do so.*
7. *Make it fully accountable, with no greater job security than exists in the private sector. Once upon a time someone set standards. Today everyone excuses their absence.*
8. *Make them sensitive to individual need - not just projecting their own needs on everyone else, and calling them outcomes.*
9. *With mutual respect, remembering that healthy respect cannot be a one-way street, that love is a bonus, and hatred the enemy.*
10. *No.*

Share your answers to these and other questions

Go to the Blog on www.DeathofaNightingale.com

The clash of human rights and "Unequal Opportunity"

Let me explain why I wrote Death of a Nightingale and why, ten years later, I republish it.

At the time, I wrote that I saw a small part of a bigger picture. I now see much more of it, especially the abuse and misuse of human rights laws. I hope that academia, lawyers and politicians will see this as a challenge. They don't always recognise that quite often human rights clash, and they should not ignore it as they habitually do

The right of rail workers to strike versus your right to work. The rights of climate protesters versus your right to use the King's Highway. The right of doctors and nurses to strike. The rights of their patients. Don't they have rights too? A thought reinforced when I looked around my fellow patients in ward 16 of the Freeman Hospital in Newcastle. The rights of cyclists versus the rights of the majority of other road users. I have seen that one at close quarters. Cycle lanes for non-existent cyclists in Newcastle and millions of pounds wasted providing them, better spent elsewhere heralding electric vehicles.

Today, people assert their rights on the basis that they are equal, absolute and beyond question. But are they? Today, when they clash with the rights of others, it is central or local government diktat, Trade Union power or individual grandstanding that decides. No one speaks out for the losers. No one demands fair play. And BBC NewsNight never seems to ask the question.

But many rights are not equal and absolute. If that is what you believe, and if you act on it, know that sometimes this can be, and it is a recipe for anarchy.

Many rights are unequal and relative. Recognise that they depend on the circumstances whether or not they can be justified. I write what follows to illustrate that. And my challenge to you, let *Three Wise Ones* decide, people with power and responsibility, like Andrew Marr, Laura Kuenssberg, and Oprah Winfrey. Let them use their professionally honed fairness here. Lawyers just don't see it. They live in a bubble of their own creation.

My story

I witnessed the clash between the right of children with special needs to mainstream education and the right of their parents to the school of their choice; both rights enshrined in Statute Law. The wrong side won. Diversity should have pre-empted Equality. It didn't. Over 100 special schools were closed in the UK.

I saw the attempt to close a very good school against the wishes of the parents, the teachers, the carers and the children themselves, and Sunderland's Medical Committee. The four consultants who used to visit their patents in the school, too. That wouldn't happen in a mainstream school!

"We believe that to lose the excellence of a school which has worked so well for so long represents a serious loss for the children of Sunderland. Once lost it is a facility which would be very difficult, if not impossible, to recreate. We urge those responsible for this decision to reconsider."

1996 OFSTED gave it glowing report

"It is a good school with many outstanding features... pupils in the school are highly motivated, eager to learn and responsive to the high expectations of their teachers ... the School's ethos is very positive. The school provides pupils with a range of opportunities within the curriculum and, through an extensive programme of links, to take an active role in a variety of social settings to prepare them for life after school. Pupils' good behaviour is an outstanding feature. When appropriate, pupils assist each other in work and leisure. Relationships with staff are very good."

But, in 1994 an international conference of 92 governments at Salamanca urged that those with special educational needs must have access to special schools with an inclusive ethos. And this was already national and local government policy in the UK at the time.

I shall illustrate the strength of the opposition to it and the amazing support they received.

However, this didn't stop the local authority in their tracks. Initially, the parents' campaign appeared to succeed, but today the school is not what it was. It meets different needs. It doesn't need hydrotherapy. Children with a physical disability and a learning difficulty in Sunderland are now in mainstream schools. Their parents will now claw at the air if they are unhappy.

Before I begin, with children's right to mainstream education the chicken came before the egg. I write this especially for students of Jurisprudence. The orgasm came when the Labour Government's Education Bill reached the House of Lords in 1976. An amendment to the bill approved then provided that right and preceded and pre-empted the Warnock Report in 1978. On page 121 Robin Jackson's explains how Inclusion was introduced in the UK.

It is amazing how for some a single word like Inclusion totally obliterates all need for an examination of detail and any contemplation of consequences; here, notably bullying and human fallibility, their own. Also, some people love to project for others what is right for themselves without caring a jot for the rights of others or knowing for a moment what they are.

And sadly, the State's ratchet applies. It never likes to own up to its own mistakes whichever Party was responsible for them, the State's diktat fuelled by ill-founded optimism, sanctioned by ill-informed media consent, and protected by non-functioning accountability. That is why fifty years later there is still a problem in search of a solution.

This is Barbara Priestman School as I knew it, with a curriculum that included music, art, and cooking, supported by physio, hydrotherapy and school nurses.

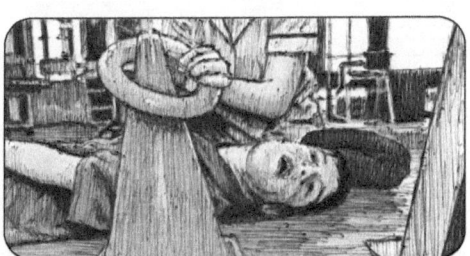

Celebrating winners, a gold medal winner at the Sidney Paralympics, a business enterprise award, the Chief Scout's Award.

Sunderland Echo-Steel Drum Band in Sedgefield

British Library - *shelfmark MFM.SP385.*

And often their Steel Drum Band was ferried around by parents for their playing engagements, here in Sedgefield, and you can see Tony Blair, their MP. They also performed at the Royal Albert Hall, in London.

When the director of education called a meeting of parents giving them the good news as he saw it that all their children were going into mainstream schools, a parent governor with two children in the school asked for a vote. Not a single hand supported the director.

The parents then mounted a campaign to stop the Labour Council closing it. They didn't go for a petition. It could be shredded. They went for reasoned objections. They had to be analysed as well as counted. And the parents secured over 14,000 of them! The Sunderland Echo lent its support as did a local advertising agency without charge.

> **Sunderland Echo -
> Keep Their Doors Open**
>
> *British Library -
> shelfmark MFM.SP385.*

> **Sunderland Echo -
> A School worth fighting for**
>
> *British Library -
> shelfmark MFM.SP385.*

The late Fredwyn Haynes, its inspiring head teacher, lent his support too in his retirement.

> **Sunderland Echo -
> Threatened School is the best there is - ex-head**
>
> *British Library -
> shelfmark MFM.SP385.*

These are the rights the parents wanted to assert in Statute:

Clause 1 (3), 2001 SEN Act: 'If a statement is maintained under section 324 for the child, he must be educated in a mainstream school <u>unless that is incompatible with - (a) the wishes of his parent</u>, or (b) the provision of efficient education for other children.' (My underlining)

One feisty pupil, Ashleigh Ritchie, now Ashleigh Watt, went on local TV and joined the lobbying in London. Here she is with Sir Tom Cowie More of her later on

The parents lobbied the Department for Education in London, including the Labour Minister, David Blunkett.

They persuaded the Minister, Charles Clarke MP to reject the local authority's proposals in their entirety.

The rights that the parents were asserting shortly afterwards were confirmed by Statute.

Clause 1 (3), 2001 SEN Act: 'If a statement is maintained under section 324 for the child, he must be educated in a mainstream school <u>unless that is incompatible with - (a) the wishes of his parent</u>, or (b) the provision of efficient education for other children.' (My underlining)

In the real world, for many children, the opportunity to go to university, equal or otherwise, is not what education is all about. It is about being the best you can be.

My great realisation in the past ten years is that this does not just relate to children with special educational needs. It relates to half the school population who fail to get into university. Do they need to have a sense of failure? This is not good for their mental health. After the suicide of their daughters, recently the *"Three Dads' Walk"* to the four Parliaments in the UK drew attention to the fact that suicide is the biggest killer of young people across the entire UK.

An article in the *Guardian* on 21 February 2021, reporting on a paper in the *British Journal of Psychiatry*, said that about 7% of children had attempted suicide by 17, and almost one in four said they self-harmed in the past year.

The figures came from an analysis of the *Millennium Cohort Study*, which followed the lives of about 19,000 young people born at the start of the millennium in England, Scotland, Wales and Northern Ireland.

Even if the writer's calculated guess that 52,427 17-year-olds attempted suicide at some point in their lives and 170,744 self-harmed in the previous 12 months is an exaggeration, it would explain why I have found this a *No Go* area for educationalists who ignored Diversity and built their policy on Inclusion and Equality, trying to be on the right side of history; and why they put all the problems in schools today down to lack of money.

Payment by achievement is a good principle in life. So pay the teaching profession a handsome reward if, in two years, they can introduce an alternative curriculum with its *5 Stars* award.

Ashleigh Ritchie has no sense of failure and never had. We were at her wedding, her teachers still her friends there. She had taken her husband to be Dance City in Newcastle to learn to dance together at her wedding, she in her wheel chair. She has just adopted a little boy. She already has two little dogs. The late Fredwyn Haynes would be proud of her. His belief was that there is nothing other kids could do that pupils in his school couldn't, given time. And that was what his school could provide that mainstream school often couldn't.

Ashleigh inspired me to create Tracy in *Death of a Nightingale*.

TRACY ON HUMAN RIGHTS LAWYERS

- I'll tell you something. Lawyers and politicians just love to give us our rights. Rights. I call them buttercups and daisies. And we are those little white dandelion heads, you know, they blow away in the wind.

Equality of opportunity is not what education should be about, certainly for all those not destined for University, not wanting to or not able to. Parity of esteem is not what it should be about either.

Self esteem. Being the best you can be. Pursuing excellence. Most people can go for that on their own terms. I saw this at Barbara Priestman School on Presentation evenings. Most kids seemed to achieve an award for something. Most notably a gold medal at the Sydney Paralympics, a scouting award, and a certificate for drawing a windmill by a girl who was blind. But not everyone can be another Helen Keller.

The late Ken Robinson who emigrated to America told this story to give the same message. In Death Valley nothing grows. It is hot, dry and lifeless. In 2004 there were 7 inches of rain in a short period of time. The following year it was a garden of flowers. The land was dormant not dead. Likewise, Education is nourishment for enquiring minds. All of them. His theme was the same as mine. One size does not fit all. Try doing it with shoes.

His wisdom:

- *If you're not prepared to be wrong, you'll never come up with anything original.*
- *In some parts of the USA, 60 percent of kids drop out of high school. In the Native American communities, it is 80 per cent of kids. If we halved that number, one estimate is it would create a net gain to the U.S. economy over 10 years of nearly a trillion dollars.*
- *If you've got two children or more, I bet you they are completely different from each other. Aren't they?*
- *The fact is that given the challenges we face, education doesn't need to be reformed —it needs to be transformed. ...*
- *Creativity is as important as literacy."*
- *Education and training are the keys to the future. A key can be turned in two directions. Turn it one way and you lock resources away; turn it other way and you realise resources and give people back to themselves.*

And Tony Blair's son Euan is much wiser than his father. He boasts that his £1.4bn business in the UK and USA promotes apprenticeships. And he uses these words: *"One of the things that's so broken about the current system is that it tries to pretend a three- or four-year undergraduate degree is enough to see you through a multi-decade career."* His father's New Labour focussed attention on getting 50% of students into university!

The message here, it is not just children with special needs that need a curriculum that they can enjoy, suitable to their needs, with exams they can pass with flying colours. Very many others. Their ambition could be to get a Five Star Award, not equal to a degree, but something they could boast wherever their lives took them, and helping them along the way. A gateway to the multiplicity of skills needed today and the jobs with them.

Here is my suggestion for their curriculum. You will have your own.

1. Computer and the Internet - no one today can exist without it. Include computer games like bridge and chess.
2. Maths including budgeting, buying and selling on credit, measuring, weighing.
3. Life skills, domestic, family. Sex. Cooking is not just a female pursuit. Understanding power supply. DIY skills. First Aid and hygiene. Love and care.
4. Music, art and design and their appreciation, the benefits to last a lifetime.
5. Sport, keeping fit and games – include Monopoly.
6. Culture including human rights, modern history, and literature including poetry and drama, and how other people in the world live. Legal stuff.
7. Two conversational foreign languages, invaluable in hospitality industry as well as in the caring professions. Yes, Mandarin Chinese an option.
8. Health and Safety – including diet to head off obesity and diabetes, PE, and sport. <u>Share responsibility for your health with the State with your watch</u>
9. Faith – understanding the world's religions – why people believe or don't – the mutuality of respect.
10. The environment – Greta Thunberg stuff even if she is a bit simplistic, only at the start of her journey.

Is there time for all this while studying for a university? And, none of it dry as dust. Start learning by doing, for life, not in books. Discover the joy that comes from creativity and giving. How much time is there for all of this in National Curriculum? Here you have "Opportunity" that doesn't have to be equal and is real.

Today it is no wonder that there are skill shortages to be met by immigration. It is no wonder kids have attention deficit hyperactivity ADHD to be treated with Ritalin. Could it be a tantrum at brain food they do not like? Some kids may need Ritalin, but multitudinous? No one had this diagnosis in my day.

Payment by achievement is a good principle in life. Pay the teaching profession a handsome reward if they can introduce a second curriculum with its 5 Stars in two years.

And loading student loans on the backs of those going to university for their lives is not a good idea either; those fixated on Equality appear to believe that if everyone can't have a bursary or a scholarship, no one should have one. Bring them back, as many as possible, especially in the medical profession as long as they don't move abroad for five years after qualifying.

I got to Oxford on a State Scholarship. Today there should be a graduate tax to pay for them, but not on the students, on the businesses and professions that will employ them and take advantage of their university learning. They could fund their own scholarships instead. They would then have a real interest in what was being taught. And the pupils themselves would have good reason to work harder at school to win one.

Put an end to student loan dependency. It diminishes more than it enables. It is a modern form of slavery.

Education, education, education. Not just the words, the deeds. Life is not about levelling. It is about achieving. Seeking excellence, not accepting mediocrity. Remember, we are equal only sometimes. We are always different.

FREEDOM OF EXPRESSION IN THE UK TODAY?

"Who Controls the Past Controls the Future." 1984 - George Orwell

In the autumn of 2008, in Sunderland, the parents of *Barbara Priestman School*, an all-age school for children with physical disabilities and a learning difficulty launched a campaign to save it from closure. The *Sunderland Echo*, then under different ownership, backed the campaign with front-page and double-page coverage. As a result, the parents secured over 14,000 reasoned objections to closure. And the campaign was a total success.

Today, however, while the school still does fine work for some children with special needs over the age of 11 with autism and serious learning difficulties, it is not the same school. And the *Sunderland Echo* is under different ownership.

What I saw then provoked me to write and stage my play *Death of a Nightingale* and publish it as well. I now write to bring the story up to date.

Today, I record the following dialogue with the present editor of the Sunderland Echo:

Can I respectfully ask you if you are aware of the current political significance of these historic photographs in relation to the human rights of parents with children with special educational needs and others. I detail this in the enclosures.

Alan

The reply:

I have just told you that I am no longer prepared to discuss this matter any further. You do not have permission to use our copyrighted materials

and no amount of messages will change this decision. Please instruct your publishers NOT to use any of our copyrighted materials as we do not authorise their use in any circumstances."

There appeared to be no complaints process, and I obtained no answer from the editor of *NationalWorld*, who owns the paper, even though I tweeted him.

As a result, I tell the story with illustrations that I commissioned my publishers to secure at some personal cost and with narrative. As you can see, prominent members of the Labour Government saw, but did not appear to understand.

My right to free expression has been restricted elsewhere.

MY ENGLAND is my autobiography. My life did not go according to plan from first to last, but it has been blessed by my family, friends, and my wife Ros. It has also been blessed by some good fortune. And I would not have reached the age of 90 without the NHS and the medical profession to whom I am profoundly indebted.

It is also a criticism of my own generation. Its hypocrisy. Its complacency and its self-satisfaction. Its waste of human and natural resources. It exposes Corporatism masquerading as Democracy with the people at the top enjoying the fruits of other people's labours. It exposes authoritarianism masquerading as socialism. It is a call to the Left to provide the conscience for capitalism and make itself electable.

I write it for future generations.

While it is titled MY ENGLAND it could just as easily be titled MY WORLD.

- The War to save Planet Earth should dwarf all other wars. Today it doesn't.
- The contention should not be between those who believe in their exclusive right to God but between those who believe in an all-inclusive God and those who do not believe at all.
- And people should see where treasure and happiness truly lie. I can give some clues.
- More than ever, a multi-cultural world needs to live at peace with itself.

In two case studies – Cycle lanes for non-existent cyclists, and equal opportunity to go to university when children with special needs and very many others simply want Opportunity - see the acceptance of mediocrity in the name of equality, authority hi-jacked, accountability non-existent, the media silent and education and the NHS badly flawed. See the tyranny of a minority and the powerlessness of the majority.

This is a call to the rising generation to play to its strengths and not be obsessed by its weaknesses. To acknowledge that we are equal only sometimes, unequal most times and always different. And an encouragement to the young to believe in themselves, pursue excellence, be the best they can be, and to own their own futures.

It wants the reader to be a Winner.

THIS BOOK CONTAINS OVER 100 IMAGES. AGAIN, MY PUBLISHERS COULD NOT OBTAIN THE CONSENT OF THE OWNERS OF THE COPYRIGHT TO MY USE OF SOME OF THEM. IT CANNOT BE PUBLISHED UNTIL THE RIGHT OF FREE EXPRESSION AIDED BY THE ORIGINALITY OF AI PRE-EMPTS THE RIGHT OF THE OWNERS OF COPYRIGHT WHEN THEY ARE PUBLISHED FOR EDUCATIONAL PURPOSES IN THE PUBLIC INTEREST

KAFKA'S CYCLE

And the Slow Death of a Complaint

Bicycles Ai Weiwei

ALAN SHARE

THIS BOOK PUTS ON THE RECORD MY FAILED ATTEMPT TO COMPLAIN ABOUT A PROPOSAL TO PUT CYCLE LANES AND RED LINES ON GOSFORTH HIGH STREET NEWCASTLE IN THE ALMOST TOTAL ABSENCE OF CYCLISTS. IT ALSO RECORDS THE SUBSTANCE OF THE COMPLAINT WITH MY OWN PHOTOGRAPHIC EVIDENCE.

Gosforth High Street is the main North/South arterial road out of Newcastle. It is also a very busy shopping street and it is very narrow. The Local Government Ombudsman rejected my complaint.

I took a 100-page dossier to leading London lawyers asking them to write a pre-action protocol letter, a necessary precursor to Judicial Review. However, they returned part of my payment saying that professionally they could not do this as it would be *"bound to fail"*.

I did not accept that my complaint was TWM, "totally without merit", and challenged their decision first with the Legal Ombudsman and then with the Solicitors Regulation Authority. My book records my failure.

Before publication I sent the book to the London lawyers indicating that I would delete anything unfair or untrue. This was their reply.

Dear Mr Share,

I confirm receipt of your 9 July 2019 letter and book.

I will not give the assurances you seek in your letter, nor will I read the book and catalogue points of disagreement. For the avoidance of any doubt, if you, or your publisher, publishes disparaging, libellous or defamatory statements of any kind about XXXXXX or the lawyers who work here, or those have formally worked on your case, you can be assured that we will avail ourselves of our legal remedies, bring legal action and seek injunctions or damages as appropriate along with the costs of doing so.

I trust this at least makes our position clear.

THIS BOOK CANNOT BE PUBLISHED UNTIL THOSE WHO WISH TO ALLEGE LIBEL MUST IDENTIFY IT.

I WROTE THIS BOOK DRAWING ON THE LESSONS I LEARNED PURSUING A CAREER THAT I HAD REJECTED IN THE COCKSURE IGNORANCE OF YOUTH

Twenty years after leaving university, a true friend told me I was getting it all wrong; and I needed a manager.

Twenty-five years afterwards, I quit the roller-coaster ride, comfortably retired with a management buyout, and let my manager and his colleagues thoroughly enjoy all the fruits of success.

Here are some of the tools of the trade I learned along the way.

The tradition of the Bar in the legal profession is to pass on home-spun wisdom, work skills and experience to the young – Pupillage. I was happy to do the same. It ill-becomes lawyers to prevent people from doing this with their time-consuming, costly, smug legal stonewalling.

YOU CAN ONLY LEARN LESSONS FROM LIVING IF OTHER PEOPLE LET YOU AND YOU SPEND SOME TIME READING THEM

HOW YOU WIN

Success certainly comes from what you know. It is impossible without it.
It will sometimes come from whom you know.
And you need a bit of luck too. Sometimes you make your own.
Strangely it does not always come from your own family. They can make you or break you.
Essentially it comes down to *YOU*. Do you know *WHERE* you are going? Do you know *HOW* you will get there?
There are lots of books telling you *WHAT* you need to know. That is the warp. This book will tell you *HOW* you get there. It is the weft.
Strategy, tactics, and the words you use. The secrets to your success.

SAY 'YES' TO LIFE

Can you hear the silence? Not mine. I have 11,505 connections on Linkedin. In particular, I refer to the Times and Times Ed.

Meanwhile, *National World* has no complaints procedure, no investigative procedure and no mind of its own.

Can your hear the silence.
something isn't right.
dead is the night.
who turn out the lights.

then they converge upon me like vulture.
a breeze of wind blows and
bring the chills right down to my very bones.
I know I'm done for but don't even care
cause its not my nightmare but yours.
twisted and turned. living on dead memories.
eating upon them so slowly.

Can you hear the silence.
something isn't right. dead is the night.
Who turned off the lights.
who is it this time.
again they converge.
but this isn't my nightmare.
its yours. watch in despair.
suck in your last bit of air.
no life left for me.
giving up and letting the leeches feed.
for everyone has their needs.
everyone needs to bleed.
and this time its you destiny.

Can you hear the silence.
something isn't right.
dead is the night.
who turned of the light.
who is it this time.
just remember this is not my nightmare but your.

you open the door welcome them in.
so now you must try to fend hyenas off if you can.
if not welcome to the damned.

Ace Of Black Hearts

NOTE POEMHUNTER.COM *Poems are the property of their respective owners. All information has been reproduced here for educational and informational purposes to benefit site visitors, and is provided at no charge...*

Bibliography

Towards Inclusive Schooling by Mel Ainscow British Journal of Special Education Volume 24 No 1 March 1997

The Role of LEAs in Developing Inclusive Policies and Practices, by Mel Ainscow, Peter Farrell, Dave Tweddle and George Malki,

Families Back Drive for Special Education Overhaul; after Warnock's Climb down. Pressure for Change The Daily Mail, June 10, 2005.

The Next Step for Special Education by Mel Ainscow, British Journal of Special Education Volume 27 No2 June 2000 *SEN and Disability Rights in Education Bill*, Consultation Document published by the DfEE, and the *2001 Act* itself.

Costs and Outcomes for Pupils with Moderate Learning Difficulties in Special and Mainstream Schools, Research Report RR89 published by DfEE December 1998

SEN Code of Practice on the Identification and Assessment of Pupils with Special Educational Needs & SEN Thresholds: Good Practice Guidance ... Consultation Papers published by the DfEE in July 2000

SEN Code of Practice DfES 581/2001, November 2001

Removing Barriers to Achievement - The Government's Strategy for SEN, DfES Publications DfES/0117/2004

The wrong debate by Alan Dyson, *Special* Spring 2000, published by NASEN. Education Act 1996

Excellence in Schools, Government White Paper published by the Stationery Office July 1997

British Journal of Special Education Volume 26 No 3 September 1999 *Educational Inclusion and Raising Standards* by Michael Farrell, British Journal of Special Education Volume 27 No1 March 2000

The Debate That Never Happened by Charles Gains and Philip Garner *Special* Autumn 2000 Published by NASEN

The Debate Begins by Philip Garner and Charles Gains, *Special* Spring 2001, published by NASEN.

Enabling Inclusion Blue Skies ... Dark Clouds? Contributions by special needs and educational professionals, The Stationery Office 2001

Leadership by Rudolph W. Giuliani, publisher, Buchet Chastel March 16, 2003

The Lord of the Flies by William Golding, Faber and Faber; New Ed edition, 1997

Hansard Report of the Second Reading of Special Educational Needs and Disability Bill in the House of Lords on 19 December 2000, and of the Grand Committee on 23 January 2001

Hansard Report of the Second Reading of the Special Educational Needs and Disability Bill in the House of Commons on 20 March 2001

Essays in Jurisprudence and Philosophy H.L.A.Hart Oxford University Press, reprinted 2001.

Forward to Ethics of Special Education K R Howe and O.B Miramontes New York by J M Kauffman Teachers College Press 1992

Whitehall's Black Box: Accountability and performance in the senior civil service Institute for Public Policy Research ISBN: 1860302998 August 2006

What does 'Inclusion' Mean for Children with Physical Disabilities, an Occasional Paper by Dr. Ann Llewellyn Special Children February 2001

Helen Keller Quotes http://thinkexist.com/quotes/helen_keller/4.html

The impact of paid adult support on the participation and learning of pupils in mainstream schools EPP December 2003 Review

Meeting Special Educational Needs - A programme of action, ISBN 085522 906 3 published 1998.

Meeting Special Educational Needs: A programme for Action DfEE, 1998

Moderate Learning Difficulties and the Future of Inclusion, Braham Norwich and Narcie Kelly. RoutledgeFalmer 2005 ISBN 0-415-31974-9

Power to the People http://www.parliament.uk/commons/lib/research/notes/snpc-03948.pdf

The Dignity of Difference: How to Avoid the Clash of Civilizations by Chief Rabbi Sir Jonathan Sacks. Publisher: Continuum International Publishing Group; 2 Sub edition July 2003

The Great Partnership – God, Science and the search for meaning by Jonathan Sacks: Hodder & Stoughton 2011

Music and the Mind by Anthony Storr, Harper Collins Publishers, 1992.

Valuing People - A New Strategy for Learning Disability for the 21st Century Cm5086 published by the Department of Health March 2001

SEN and Disability Green Paper Department for Education March 2011

William Armstrong, Magician of the North – Henrietta Heald, Northumbria Press, 2010

Toolkit of Strategies to Improve Learning - Summary for Schools Spending the Pupil Premium Sutton Trust May 2011

Food and Faith: Amazon.co.uk: Susan Reuben, Sophie Pelham: Books 2011

A Testimonial of Substance

Sir Iain Glidewell PC
(8 June 1924 – 8 May 2016) Lord Justice of Appeal

> ROUGH HEYS FARM
> HENBURY
> MACCLESFIELD
> CHESHIRE SK11 9PF
> 01625 614379
> 1st February 2008
>
> Alan Share Esq.
>
> Dear Alan,
>
> Thank you for sending me your splendid book. I have read it with interest and admiration. You are much to be congratulated, particularly because you have thrown yourself so wholeheartedly into the campaign to alter Government policy towards the education of children with special needs. I am sure that without you, the situation would be worse than it is. I believe that sometimes in my judicial career I had the opportunity to do some good, but I have never taken up a particular cause in the way you have, and I admire you for it.
>
> Thank you too for your reference to CNG in the preface. I have always been conscious how much I owe him. Once, when I had been in silk a few years, he cautioned me against becoming too establishment minded. I hope I took it to heart.
>
> With all good wishes,
>
> Ever yours,
> Iain

His father, CN Glidewell, head of planning chambers in Manchester, my pupil master. Liberal ppc Clitheroe 1929

Dear Alan

Thank you for sending me your book. I have read it with interest and admiration. You are to be congratulated particularly because you have thrown yourself so wholeheartedly into the campaign to alter Government policy towards the education of children with special needs. I am sure that without you the situation would be worse than it is. I believe that sometimes in my judicial career I had the opportunity to do some good work, but I have never taken up a particular cause in the way you have, and I admire you for it.

Thank you for your reference to CNG in the preface. I have always been conscious how much I owe him. Once, when I had been in silk a few years, he cautioned me against being too establishment minded. I hope I took it to heart.

With all good wishes,

Yours ever,
Iain

Alan Share

For over 17 years a governor of a special school for children with a physical difficulty and an associated learning difficulty, chair of governors for most of that time.

A degree in Jurisprudence at Merton College, Oxford. A barrister, practiced for only three years and left the Bar to work for the Liberal Party in London. After that headed up and grew a retail furniture company in NE England. Active in his trade association, played a lead role in the design of Flammability labels for sofas. A director of the British Shops and Stores Association and chair of a nationwide committee that set up the Qualitas Conciliation for the Furniture and Carpet Industry, now the Furniture Ombudsman.

For many years, chair of the board of a residential care home in Newcastle. In recent years chair of TYDFAS, the Newcastle branch of the National Association of Decorative and Fine Arts Societies. A member of his local Rotary Club, seeing this book and his involvement in Special Needs as acts of Rotary service.

Travels widely, enjoys music and the arts and is never, ever bored.

If Great Britain had surrendered to Hitler, his life would have ended long ago in a gas chamber along with millions of others. Were it not for the medical profession and the NHS he would not be here today. Were it not for his teachers his life would not have been so rewarding. He sees *Death of a Nightingale* as a way of expressing his thanks.

In June 2008 "Featured Author" of the month - Oxford Alumni and Blackwell publishers.

www.ingramcontent.com/pod-product-compliance
Lightning Source LLC
LaVergne TN
LVHW040143080526
838202LV00042B/3003